THE STORY OF AXEL MUNTHE

E·P·DUTTON & CO. INC
1852 — 1953
CREATIVE · 101 YEARS · PUBLISHING

Axel Munthe through the entrance of the Tower of Materita, Capri

THE STORY
OF
AXEL MUNTHE

By GUSTAF MUNTHE

and

GUDRUN UEXKÜLL

Translated from the Swedish
by Malcolm Munthe and from
the German by Lord Sudley

NEW YORK

E. P. DUTTON & CO., INC.

1953

INTRODUCTION by MALCOLM MUNTHE

THE ONLY REASON I HAVE BEEN ASKED TO INTRODUCE THIS book is that Axel Munthe was my father.

I hope this disclosure will not be a disappointment to that wide circle of my father's admirers who persisted in considering him as a bachelor even when they had known him for years. Once, before the war, when my aunt introduced me, at the age of 19, to a witty and famous London hostess, she exclaimed, " But this must be six foot of mirage because I've known Axel Munthe all my life, and he just couldn't be married!" The crowded salon laughed and the " mirage " turned crimson and wondered where birth certificates were kept. At school, after *The Story of San Michele* became a best-seller, masters or parents of school-fellows would often ask " . . . your uncle?" but never " . . . your father?" For many, Axel Munthe, ' the Svengali of modern times ', was a forlorn bachelor relegated by the cruelty of his blindness to a crumbling castle on the crest of Capri—no family man, with a wife as beautiful as she was good and two large boys; no hearth with a bright fire in it, and slippers!

So it has to be admitted that by asking one of the sons to write an Introduction, the publisher of this book—my father's old friend Sir John Murray—is preparing to shatter a widely held illusion.

Father was married, and, in that, the brilliant London hostess of my youth was wrong. Father was utterly lonely to the end and in that she was right.

If he was unconventional as a husband, he was just as much so as a father. But he knew how to be a friend beyond compare. And when his faithful luck found him at last an intelligent partner in marriage, strong enough to survive the scorching of his temperament, it was this quality of friendship which must have saved for all eternity what no laws of Church or State could have bound for a single year.

Axel Munthe needed to own a family just as he needed to own San Michele. Long after he had ceased to want to live there he was still unable to let it go out of his ownership. He asked only to know that his goods and chattels were there, and that they were still his. He did not even want to be proud of them with his friends. He preferred to return to admire his San Michele alone, almost by stealth; just as, alone, he liked to return to find his family. He never wanted to show his friends the wife he thought so beautiful. Behind a high wall in a garden alone with her he would pick a pale English rose and silently hold it against the soft cheek it resembled. He was a collector, but he never showed off his collection. As to his sons, he never insisted on showing them off either, and, fortunately, he did not require them to be bright.

I can remember him once coming home after a long absence and when my brother came into the room he patted him on the shoulder and said half to himself, " English shoulders." I know now that he felt proud at that moment. Later, after the War, when he was old, sitting in his chair talking to us, he would blindly fumble his long bony fingers in my hair and feel for the wound and mutter, " That's the best decoration you could have, boy." And the old, militant lover of down-trodden humanity would forget himself so far as to say, " My sons are serving in the British forces." The ownership, not the son, gave him at that moment a touch of pride.

Full of inconsistencies, yet simple as home-made bread, this strange, ungovernable creature, when once he came into the orbit of some life, took a great deal of room in it, and when he left an emptiness remained.

Introduction

The perfect biography would have to explain all that, and the idea of a detailed " life " was carefully examined by his family when, soon after his death, would-be biographers appeared. The papers were sorted. There are drawers and trunks full of letters, crumpled and faded, covering half a century and more, in five languages. Photographs of mutely staring faces, some with names on the back, others without, silently keeping the secret. There are objects—gifts from patients, gifts from friends, souvenirs of moments which meant something to him ? There are still today, happily, those who know their meaning and who remember. However, though the idea of a full biography was for the present abandoned, this little book is nevertheless a beginning for which some may be grateful.

1953

Contents

★ These chapters are by Gudrun Uexküll.

[ix]

Contents

Illustrations

Illustrations

PREFACE by GUSTAF MUNTHE

THE FACT THAT AXEL MUNTHE DESCRIBED HIMSELF AND his life so well and so vividly in *The Story of San Michele* makes it difficult to write his biography. It would seem almost hopeless to try and throw further light on a life which, with its many facets, was constantly in the lime-light.

Now that he is dead, however, one may appear justified with the aid of memories and impressions in venturing upon a modest description of his life and personality, if only for the sake of the many millions who were captivated by his book.

He himself honestly admits that in his own *Story of San Michele* and earlier works he has mingled truth and imagination. From the standpoint of immortality that is of no account, and does not affect his importance as a writer. But it has helped to give his personal character a trait of unreality, and people have in consequence formed completely contra-dictory impressions of Munthe as a man.

I do not claim that my description of him is any truer than those written by others, especially as I knew him personally only during the last years of his life, but it may contribute to the detailed study of his life and work which is bound to appear sooner or later.

I am greatly indebted to Ludwig and Ake Wilson Munthe's book *The Munthe Clan in Sweden*, and to the family archive deposited in the Swedish Royal Archives for my chapter on Axel Munthe's family and childhood. And I would like here to express my deep gratitude to all who have helped to bring this book to light.

PREFACE by GUDRUN UEXKÜLL

ANY READERS OF *The Story of San Michele* MUST HAVE asked themselves: " What is this man Axel Munthe really like? Even though we may never meet him personally it would be interesting to know how much truth and how much fiction there is in the extraordinarily fascinating portrait he draws of himself in every page of his book."

Those intent on finding out what they call the ' truth ' about him should start with the maxim which Axel Munthe invented in a foreword to his book, and which most readers have entirely overlooked: " Ce n'est rien donner aux hommes que de ne pas donner soi-même."

Perhaps that is the answer to the sceptics, whose thoughts he had already divined before putting pen to paper. For what does the word ' perception ' really mean? If it means " what I know from what my senses have told me "; then the sum of both knowledge and sensation merely provides a picture of the world peculiar to, and only recognizable by, single individuals; each of us creating for himself his whole world from a jumble of confusing details by observing and interpreting what he sees.

Is it not always a Self that perceives, either objectively or subjectively? I believe that when Axel Munthe wrote his book he wanted to present us with this self. Moreover, even the least imaginative of men must ' imagine ' a little to make a significant and consistent ' whole ' of his experiences.

Munthe knew that he saw more in things than the average man, and when he allowed us a glimpse of the rich content of his mind he was aiming at something better than a dull record of facts.

Whether he gives his characters a background of dazzling sunshine or of melancholy twilight, they are always the creations of an artist. True, many of them are borrowed from his dreams and nourished by his fantasies and longings. In his preface he says candidly that we must not always believe him, and enquires whimsically whether life is ever true.

His cousin Gustaf Munthe's part of this biography will be particularly welcome to all who wish to know more of Axel Munthe and the actual events of his life. My own contribution is mainly a personal record of the last years of Axel's life, and certain impressions of his earlier years.

" I'm a queer fish," he used to say, whenever he surprised or enraged anyone. It was a form of excuse for anything which he could not reduce to a common denominator, himself included. He regarded even himself as one of the many puzzles which he pondered over in his lonely hours. He sometimes spoke of himself as a savage, referring to his carefree unconventionality which often astonished and annoyed people.

Indeed, he often actually enjoyed annoying people; it provided a good opening for his never-failing sense of humour. And yet, when he wanted, he could be unusually formal and correct, but then his innate courtesy transformed this conventionality into an expression of genuine feeling.

It was as though the two points of the compass, north and south, had presided like goddesses of fate at his christening. Axel Munthe's character was half fierce and stormy like the Goths and Vikings of his native land, half mild like the Grecian sky and the warmth of southern summers. It was rare to find a man so vital and yet so contradictory—his mind an ever-swinging pair of scales, with golden trays too amply laden. With his strong drive to assert himself and to ignore convention, he forced his way through life like a geyser bursting through unyielding granite.

Poor and not particularly robust, he was faced early in life with obstacles which he had to surmount. Someone who knew him then compared him to a stormy north wind. Forthright and violent, he would brook no opposition, and even though unconvinced, people always gave way to him. Early in life he must have had an intuitive knowledge of his own destiny, and it was this inner sense which caused so many of his friends to fly to him for advice in solving their own problems and, indeed, to honour him almost as a seer.

Little is known of his boyhood, but we can almost imagine we knew him then, when from time to time he gives us glimpses of that state of *puer aeternus*. He must have been very lonely, and perhaps that loneliness was the shield which the gods grant to those they love, to help them to fulfil their life tasks unhampered by daily cares, and to avoid anything that could lead them astray. Protected by this shield, the heart receives the accolade of nobility, and in the quiet of loneliness learns its mission and calling. This knowledge of his destiny, acquired early in life, also gave Axel Munthe the drive which enabled him—even before he embarked on his own special calling—to outdistance his contemporaries in work, both at school and at the university.

In those days Fate seemed to hold out even more dazzling prospects for him. Work, success, art and the gift of making friends were all his for the taking. And yet in spite of the rush and bustle of those years of forging ahead, two saints seem to have been his constant, invisible companions. They were familiar to him from his childhood's dreams: St. Michael the champion against the powers of darkness, bold and proud in his glittering armour, and St. Francis of Assisi, in his drab habit, humble in his love for all God's creatures.

These two saints have no doubt made their peace in Heaven long ago, though here on earth we find countless instances in which they seem almost to ignore each other. They can exist side by side only in a career such as that of Axel Munthe, though there may have been many incidental clashes between the three.

Pride and meekness, strife and tranquillity—truly notable guests in the narrow dwelling of a single heart! No wonder that heart was restless; no wonder Axel Munthe spent many a sleepless night.

Treasures of worldly wisdom, strung on the golden thread of fond recollection, are to be found in Munthe's book *The Story of San Michele*. Years ago it first set off on its peaceful career of conquest round the world, and millions have admired and delighted in it. It has wrung tears of joy and also, like a divining-rod, tears of pity from the most stony-hearted.

One of its best critics said of the book: " It was written to combat sleeplessness, and disturbs the sleep of the world."

Prologue: The Hermit of Stockholm Palace

FIVE YEARS, ALMOST TO A DAY, BEFORE HIS DEATH I CALLED upon Axel Munthe at the Palace in Stockholm for the first time. The war had driven him from his beloved Capri and King Gustaf had invited him as his guest to the Palace. His visit was never intended to be more than a temporary measure, but gradually, as the years went by, the stay was prolonged.

His rooms were in the south wing on the first floor and they overlooked the formal seventeenth-century Palace garden on one side and the harbour close by Slottsbacken on the other. The way up to his apartments through this vast old labyrinth was long and tortuous. From the great courtyard one entered the doors of the east arcade and wandered along a gallery lined with eighteenth-century reproductions of Greek statues, then past the old Palace well and up a worn stone staircase to a long, stone-flagged corridor. Many doors gave off the corridor and on one of these was a card : " Axel Munthe ".

The rooms were quaint; low ceilings, deep window recesses, old china stoves in the corners and picturesque old furniture. He was usually to be found sitting in a monumental armchair by the writing-table in the middle of the room with a rug over his knees. He was tall and thin and wore his grey beard cut short to a point and his hair lanky and unkempt. His spectacles had a dark glass over his blind eye. He seemed to neglect his appearance entirely, partly no doubt on account of his failing eyesight but partly also from a dimly conscious vanity.

At the time of which I write he was already a very old, tired and sick man. Though he had regained the use of one eye after an operation some years earlier he still saw very little and was extremely sensitive to strong light. But he could recognize people and managed to read and write a little. What seemed to distress him most was his asthma and the ills that went with it, especially on hot summer nights when each breath was anguish. One by one the ailments of old age were laying siege to him at last.

He was not the type of man to bear his cross with patience; he grumbled incessantly. Being a doctor himself, he could not resist the temptation to diagnose his various symptoms; and though he delighted in stating his contempt for doctors in general, including himself, he enjoyed discussing his condition with other men of medicine. He liked to observe the action of his own heart with the aid of the modern cardiogram apparatus.

In those days I used to see him about twice a week. He would telephone when he felt lonely and wanted company, and at such moments he would view his friend's appointments or convenience with a truly royal indifference. One evening when he was trying to get hold of me by telephoning to my home at about 7.30 he was told I was out. "What!" he peevishly muttered, "does he always run around on the loose at nights?" Sometimes he would ask me to stay to a meal. His food was served from the Palace kitchens and, as he ate very little himself, there was always plenty for at least one unexpected guest. Occasionally he would drink a glass of wine and enjoyed a certain old and much-coveted vintage of Madeira which the Palace cellars could provide. Towards the end, after he had given up taking his meals at table, one of these dusty and ancient bottles might sometimes be seen on the writing-desk beside him, and with all the deference born of appreciation he would offer his visitor a glass. But his life was frugal in the extreme and at last, when his roamings became restricted to his apartments in the palace, he seemed to subsist almost entirely on milk foods.

For several years he had employed, as help and general factotum, Vittorio, the son of his old Italian housekeeper at Capri, an arrangement which in due course was to become increasingly irksome to both parties. Axel Munthe was, like many aged people, an unregenerate despot and required constant attention. Vittorio found this somewhat of a strain and soon reached the conclusion that Court life did not fully come up to his expectations. I did what I could to persuade the old man to release Vittorio and there was considerable relief all round when I was finally permitted to order his tickets back to Capri. Munthe had resisted stubbornly, and when he finally gave in it seemed as if he was giving up something more as well. He had only one and a half years of life left to him.

A young Red Cross sister, Brita Elmgren, was engaged to look after him and she can scarcely have found her task any easier than Vittorio had found his, so exacting had her patient become. If she was away from his side for a bare hour he would find it much too long. " Do you suppose she is out dancing, or what?" he would ask with a guileful expression in his eye, if the poor woman so much as slipped away to wash her hair. But a great change was discernible from the days when he had ordered the unfortunate Vittorio to and fro, and though he might grumble now and then the new arrangement suited him better on the whole.

One outward and visible sign of the new régime was his improved appearance. The old, utterly indescribable clothes he had treasured so long disappeared one by one and he took to wearing, mostly, a smart dressing-gown, given to him by the King as a Christmas present. His beard was now neatly trimmed.

In earlier years he was often to be seen wandering about the town, sometimes on his own, sometimes leaning on the arm of

Vittorio or some old friend. He liked poking about the narrow alley-ways of the Old Town, and wherever he went he made friends with the inhabitants, humans and animals alike. He kept an especially warm place in his heart for the aged poor of Stockholm's Old Town, and these he tried to help on many occasions.

This special affection of his for the Old Town was not only because it was near: the dark alley-ways and their shady inhabitants attracted him just as they had done earlier in Italy's poorest quarters. The artificial, strictly fenced-in world to which he originally belonged gave too little scope for his passionate longing to feel the beating pulse of real life and living art, the things which seemed to him beautiful and exciting. His whole being craved brightest sun as well as deepest shade, the widest possible range of moods and emotions to play upon. His imagination was very powerful, but it needed material with which to build. An unknown figure threading an uncertain way through crowds and disappearing down a street could, provided it touched his sense for the peculiar and picturesque, become a whole story in all its detail. Even when he no longer had the strength to translate it into words, it still made the substance of his daily life. The stranger need not be human; a cat vanishing round the corner of a house, a geranium in a high window, a piece of stick floating like a galleon in a gutter or even the specks of sunshine sparkling through the leaves of a tree in the depths of a gloomy courtyard could tempt his imagination.

Outings became shorter. I would stroll with him around the immediate precincts of the Palace. Later the great court-yard became the limit of our walk, and here he liked to listen to the music during the changing of the guard. Our main preoccupation was to get as far as possible into the warming sunshine without letting its harsh rays pierce his aching eye. So little by little even the great courtyard had to be abandoned

[4]

and only the east arcade remained, in which he would march slowly backwards and forwards. Every now and again he would stop to say a word to one of his friends amongst the Palace porters or to turn an unseeing gaze out towards the golden view of the harbour beyond the Logard garden. Often in the years of his strength when he suffered from long spells of insomnia he used to get up from his bed, dress hastily and wander about at night for hours in those echoing arcades.

Slowly but surely the day was approaching when he could no longer go out at all. Then even he recognized what a big step he had taken towards the inevitable.

These long slow walks in the great courtyard and the arcades were very monotonous for him, for his mind worked with amazing clarity right up to his death, even if at times it was too tired to work uninterruptedly through a whole day. His memory was astonishing, and if momentarily it failed him his tremendous power of invention always came to the rescue.

He was a fascinating raconteur. His mind could roam at will over an immensely wide field of knowledge, covering personal experiences, world politics, everything under the sun from the froth at the surface down to the deepest mysteries of life. His judgment was clear, often harsh, and he had very decided likes and dislikes.

He dreaded losing the full keenness of his brain. He hated the long snowbound northern winters and longed for the fertile warmth of his Capri. He adored life, the sun, above all things. So it must have seemed to him the most senseless irony of an unkind Fate that the all-healing light and warmth of the sun should turn on him and pierce his eye and suffocate his lungs when he needed them most.

The House of Munthe and Childhood

AXEL MUNTHE WAS DESCENDED FROM A MEDIAEVAL Flemish family of rank, who owned property at Munte, a small village, five kilometres from Ghent, which still bears that name.

The family trace back an unbroken line from father to son through eleven hundred years. Down the pages of mediaeval history they appear as Knights, Crusaders to the Holy Land, Abbots at St. Peter's, Courtiers at the Holy Roman Imperial Courts in Flanders, and as landowners.

The last of this line of Roman Catholic noblemen to live in Flanders became disastrously involved in the religious wars which harassed Europe in the sixteenth century. Adam of Munthe was a general in the Emperor Charles V's army. His Protestant son Ludovic had to escape through Germany to Lübeck, and in 1580 settled as a merchant in Copenhagen. Ludovic's elder son Hans became Protestant Bishop of Bergen in Norway and the younger son, Arnold, became Professor of Theology at Lund University, and there he lies buried in the Cathedral in the Dionysi Chapel. With the cession of the province of Scania to Sweden the family adopted Swedish nationality.

The descendants of this line seem to have been mostly men of learning or soldiers. Meagre signs of literary or artistic talent appear from time to time in Axel's own branch of the family. His great grandfather, who was the original on which the hero of the old Swedish folk song *Borgmastare Munthe* was modelled, was born in 1729 and died in 1795. As Mayor of Eksjo and Member of Parliament he played a typically rococo part in politics during Gustaf III's reign. In 1765 he came out as an ardent supporter of the revolutionary 'Cap' party; he worked frantically against its more extreme policy but was nevertheless arrested in 1772 when the King became fearful of Munthe's influence against the planned *coup d'état*. Later reinstated, if tradition is to be believed, after secret meetings with the King in the famous Gyldene Freden beer-cellar, he worked ever more closely with him until he ended up as his warmest supporter in the 1786 Parliament.

In that year, having sampled pretty well the whole gamut of political shades, he retired to his estates at Kvarnarp, perhaps because there was nothing left to sample. He flung his energies into agriculture and at the request of the Royal Academy of Arts and Sciences filled in his remaining days compiling a not unresourceful *Farmers' Manual*.

The old folk-song, or nursery rhyme, was intended as a political lampoon about the new Member of Parliament Munthe setting out for Stockholm laden with his impedimenta, wife, servant and all down to the family chaplain and "Young Master Carl" who

> "for a saddle was too small
> and in the chaise had to follow them all."

Carl was later to become King's Counsellor and a pioneer of fire insurance in Sweden.

Carl's brother, Jacob Ludovic, Axel's grandfather, did his best to carry on the family's military traditions with all the adventures and vicissitudes that those dashing times could offer. That he had much option in choosing his career seems unlikely for, as custom prescribed, he was posted to a regiment of Bohuslan's Green Dragoons at the tender age of 12. But the little boy survived and next appears as Adjutant of his cavalry regiment, aged 19, sallying forth to his first battle in 1789. Shortly afterwards, Gustaf III discovered that he badly needed men for his depleted fleet so, no doubt to the amazement of the young cavalry officer, he was peremptorily transferred to sea. Therefore with waves beneath his feet instead of a horse between his legs, he saw tempestuous action off the southern coast of Oland Island. It was not long, however, before his regiment was to suffer a further transformation. With the new reign Gustaf Adolf IV had them re-embodied as Smaland's Light Dragoons, and in 1806 they landed on the German coast to fight the French. Jacob Ludovic endured many escapades until he is shown as retiring in a blaze of glory and wounds, "which rendered it difficult for him to sit on horseback". That these unfortunate wounds were no reflection on his valour is borne out by the fact that he died in 1822 in the most honourable sinecure post of Master of the Royal Game Preserves of Kalmar. He had by then acquired the house at Vimmerby in which his widow was to carry on a harassed existence with ten children and very diminished resources.

Her six daughters and four sons must have been a source of anxiety and sorrowful reflection. Of her sons, one became a soldier, like his father; one went to sea in a Dutch East India merchantman which capsized in a storm that drowned all on board; one chose a legal career, but at twenty-four was swept off by the deadly cholera epidemic of 1830. The youngest, Martin Arnold Frederick, was a seedy little boy of six when his parent died: he was to be the father of Axel Munthe.

The accident of his tardy birth into so large a family made it painfully clear to everyone that he had neither expectations nor patrimony. His health was bad: his chief interest, which seems to have shown itself from the first, was in obscure books on the chemical sciences. His studies at Linkoping were apparently brought to an untimely conclusion, but he contrived to continue his chemistry under the celebrated Berzelius who presided at his examination in 1840. In 1866 he left Vimmerby to continue his work in Stockholm, but chronic bad health and a disease of the kidneys obliged him to lead a very retired existence until his death in 1877. Though the last years of his life were comparatively happy, his childhood and youth had been a struggle for survival. As a pale, anaemic schoolboy we see him feverishly scraping together pennies to pursue his beloved chemistry by lighting fires in the rooms of his richer school-fellows. Later, as a student apprentice, we see him sleeping at night in a laboratory on the narrow bench, hard and draughty but redolent of every kind of chemical concoction. His only other hobby was music, and he prac-tised with agonizing diligence on his fiddle. This, however, seems to have been more than his strict old master could stand, and young Munthe was relegated to the woodshed which was, we are told rather pathetically, " a little cold, especially in winter ". From chemistry he acquired a passion for dabbling in medicine, which he was to pass on to his younger son.

Martin Frederick found time in his short uneasy life to marry twice. The first marriage came to grief and ended in a divorce after only one year. He then married Louisa Aurora Ugarsky. Aurora, with her beautiful hands and intelligent face, bore him three children, each of whom was to become noteworthy in some walk of life.

Anna was the eldest, born in 1854. From the earliest years she showed artistic talent, and her sorrow was great when her mother forbade her to study painting at the Academy. Her next dream, the theatre, met with still less understanding, and finally she had to content herself with taking singing lessons, which pastime presumably seemed a little less abandoned in the eyes of ' Society '. But this concession failed to satisfy her and she obstinately persisted in ' messing about ' with paint until, to everyone's concern, her portrait of her father was accepted at the Art Society's Annual Exhibition.

At twenty-one she married Reinhold Norstedt the painter.

Whether her artistic development was in fact assisted by this union with the already famous young painter is doubtful, but she continued with her art and soon formed her own particular style. From portraiture she went over to flower painting, until in time she concentrated on those often small and exquisitely sensitive canvases by which she is best known and is represented in the National Museum and other galleries throughout Sweden. She remained spontaneous, charming and unpractical throughout her life. Flowers and animals held her most lasting affection. The love of animals which the world associates with Axel's name was even more uncompromising in his sister. When she became a widow for the second time (she married Frans Siberg after Norstedt's death), she devoted her life entirely to her animals, and her rooms were always filled with dogs, cats and parrots. Out in the courtyard when the winter was at its coldest and bleakest she would carefully arrange little reserves of food for tame mice or shivering rats.

The elder of her two brothers, Arnold, became a naval officer, sailed the seven seas and saw the world. For three years he was attached to the French Imperial Fleet serving in Mediterranean and Far Eastern waters. Later he served in the Swedish Fleet until at an early age he retired from active service on account of ill health with the rank of Captain. He settled down to writing naval histories and produced the *Swedish Naval Heroes* series which is now an accepted textbook in the service.

His most successful literary work was his last book, *Charles XII and the Russian Navy*. Here he strongly disputes the traditional blind acceptance of the King's infallibility, and without underestimating Charles XII's generalship he tries to show the disastrous shortcomings of his statesmanship. In 1920 the Academy of Science awarded him the Letterstedt Prize and shortly before his death in 1927 he was given the

singular distinction for a military man, of becoming Honorary
Doctor of Philosophy at Uppsala University.

In his old age, Arnold tried his versatile hand at yet another
art, play-writing. With characteristic energy he produced
Magnus Stenbok, Magdalena Rudenskiold and *The March over the
Belt* in quick succession and soon became a popular playwright
for the Swedish theatre.

Though he had only taken up the theatre as a hobby, late
in life, it seems to have interested him even as a child. He
was a leading light in the little company of five children,
Arnold, Anna, " Little Axel " and the two brothers Ranft (of
whom Albert was later to become famous as an actor-
manager), deep in the Swedish country-side. With home-
made scenery, tinsel, and much brave ranting, they acted
dramas to rend the heart, nearly one hundred years ago.

In the 1920's Arnold was a well-known figure in Stockholm.
By then the dashing young naval officer had become stocky
with bristly white hair and beard, usually to be found poring
over books in the Royal Library or walking of an evening
along Strandvagen, the fashionable parade by the water's edge.
In outward appearance he was the conventional old sailor, as
stuffy and correct as could be desired, but underneath the mask
there would seem to have been a fund of humour, fantasy and
lust for adventure second only to that of his younger brother.
The mask was perhaps as irksome to the wearer as it was to the
younger brother who mercilessly caricatures the rigid officer
Arnold in the " Corpse Conductor " chapter of *The Story of
San Michele*.

*   *   *

Axel Munthe was born at Oskarshamn in Sweden on the
31st of October 1857.

In childhood he was a pale, fair-haired boy with a rickety
constitution, speaking indistinctly with a noticeable lisp,

delighting in stuffed birds, collecting old skulls and bones, exploring the stables and making friends with all horses and dogs. He also had an uncomfortable weakness for snakes, lizards, beetles and insects, and several times he was caught trying to help a perturbed hen to hatch her eggs by sitting on them himself for long hours on end; but the result was always disastrous.

A manuscript of Arnold's gives us a depressing picture of the boyhood of the two brothers. They seem to have reacted strongly against the rather pompous solemnity of the mid-nineteenth-century Swedish home and the gloom which hung around their schools. Holidays seem to have been worst of all if the episodes described by Arnold's normally accurate pen are to be trusted. To take only one instance—the joyous holiday planned by his careful parents in the summer of 1865. The whole family proceeded to a watering-place called Sodra Vi, a tiny community of dyspeptics existing in a distant and dingy forest under the strictest routine prescribed by the local physician. Though Arnold was nine and Axel only eight, they had to accompany the rest of the family in their repeated daily visits to that chilly spring, starting at six in the morning to drink as much water as they could possibly hold and then promenading uneasily for a quarter of an hour before, one imagines, beating a hasty retreat to their lodgings. Not until nine were they allowed any breakfast, and even then the meal consisted only of plain porridge with water and a drop or two of wine instead of milk, to be eaten with hard ryebread barely scraped with butter. After this dissipation they returned in procession to the well to start the water-drinking operation all over again until it was time for lunch, a veritable orgy, we are told, of boiled fish and stewed fruit! The evening meal well maintained this standard.

After surviving this summer holiday for some days the two little boys quietly decided to run away home. They each secured a sandwich, and with no other luggage they made for the great highway, creeping along the bottom of a deep ditch as they passed the loathed spring and mumbling prayers to keep themselves in heart, their clothes torn by brambles and their consciences pricked by growing doubts.

They soon fell in with a tramp who gladly helped them to dispose of their sandwiches. After walking for many hours, very weary and dusty, they reached the outskirts of Vimmerby and were beginning to talk hopefully about the good meal and long sleep they were sure to find at their aunt's house when they were startled to hear the sound of a horse and carriage thundering up behind them. They looked back and, though still in the distance, there could be no mistaking the driver. In silence their father picked them up, sat them in the carriage beside him and drove back to Sodra Vi, where they were put to bed without any supper. Next morning the resident doctor, who seems to have been a man of some sense, declared they had all had enough water and might well return home, which they did.

The following summer holiday was more dashing. They went abroad to Copenhagen. One unlucky day the boys persuaded their parents to let them explore the city on their own in the company of their cousin Fabian. They started off, promising to be back in good time for lunch. But the three boys could not agree which sights should be visited first. Arnold said the thing most worth visiting was the port with the great ships all along the quayside. Axel knew better because he had heard of a shop with stuffed birds in the window, and Fabian was equally sure that the obvious thing to see first was the changing of the Guard in the Royal Palace Square. As it was impossible to see all three sights at once they decided to separate and do their visiting independently. In due course, without any idea of the passage of time, they returned to the hotel one by one. Here they quickly concluded that trouble was on its way, because the porter told them that the rest of the family were all out hunting the town for them. To make matters worse, the food hampers were locked up so there was nothing to do but wait in fearful anticipation. Once again they were put to bed without any supper, having already missed their lunch and tea.

Axel was ten when he started school in Stockholm. For the next five years he was to drift through the dreary stages of his education, expending as little energy as possible on his studies until one day his schoolmaster informed the worried father that, at his present rate of progress, Axel would certainly never pass his examination. It was evident that the boy had not looked at a single school book for months and had long ago decided that the entire institution, the masters, the boys, were all deadly dull. When questioned, he frankly confessed this to his father and at the same time suggested a sporting bargain—that if he were allowed to skip the remaining classes at school and were given 200 crowns, he would promise to take private lessons and matriculate within one year. Oddly enough, the father agreed to his son's proposal. Axel was as good as his word, and in the following year at the early age of sixteen he passed his matriculation with honours.

His father had his own very considerable sense of humour, and in spite of his chronic ill health and puritanical beliefs he knew how to enjoy himself in his own quiet way and could be excellent company within his small homely circle. And perhaps the strict, tidy, puritanical father had more understanding than he cared to show, or than his son divined when he described, in his chapter on Lapland in *The Story of San Michele*, the hard, tyrannical father of all time. Probably few mid-nineteenth-century fathers would have considered Axel either a conventional or a creditable son, with his regrettable egg-hatching competitions, his grizzly collection of skeletons

[14]

Arnold　　　　　　　　　　　　　　　*Axel*

Anna

Axel Munthe, his brother and sister, Stockholm, 1870

From a portrait by Ernst Josephson, 1881   *From a photograph*

Axel Munthe

and now his contagiously flippant attitude towards all recognized education.

Considering his boyhood as a whole, Axel probably enjoyed his home life. When he was fourteen he wrote to his brother, at sea:

" BELOVED BROTHER! !

I am now home from Malma, and believe me it was not as good fun as you might think, there. Home is best after all said and done—don't you agree? I have not yet caught you up in lessons by a long way. We've been on maths mostly, I haven't read a word of French and in Latin and Euclid I've only reached the 45th proposition. That's all I've managed. Towards the end of term I began to feel really homesick for father and mother and you, but soon I hope you'll be coming home as strong as a giant. I suppose by now you are a thoroughly efficient sailor? Linda's brother whom you thought was at sea has come back. He's been far away in the West Indies. The canaries have had a chick, already fully grown now, and the henbird is laying again for the fourth time. . . . When do you suppose you are coming home? I shall now close—until next letter,

Signing myself, Your ever affectionate brother
A. M. F. MUNTHE, AXEL."

In this letter he can hardly be said to have justified the reputation he later enjoyed in his family circle of being an amusing letter-writer.

As one turns over the pages of many of the old letters one can still savour the strong, undoubting, Protestant-Christian air which must have hung over that home. There is one written by their mother in 1878 to her children which they were to read only after her death:

" Anna, Arnold, and Axel, read these few words and bear

them in mind. Here are my thanks for the joy you have given me, for all you have been to me! Remember always to watch and pray God to help you, never doubt the existence of the Saviour. In His mediation lies our hope of salvation. Forgive me if I may have seemed at times too strict in my constant injunctions to you. Know that it was my love, I am so anxious for you; the many terrible stories about Life and its temptations, of which I have heard tell, make me so anxious for you. Never hurt people's feelings, for such actions will always in the end return to punish you. Be gentle, not impatient, keen to criticise yourself rather than others. Always avoid making a mountain out of a molehill, and you three children live together in peace and give each other good counsel and accept gratefully such advice. Try always to be as good as your word.

      Your mother, loving even in death,

                 Aurora Louisa Munthe."

Each in his or her own way the three children were to be influenced by the rigid faith in which they were brought up. When their father died in 1877, Axel received a letter from his elder brother, the naval officer, containing these words of consolation: " Now father's sufferings are over at last, and surely he is walking close beside us as an angel, protecting us."

So Axel's childhood and boyhood passed, in the close company of five very strongly developed characters. The wayward, charming, unpractical sister; the versatile sailor and writer brother; the retiring, firmly believing mother; the autocratic, hot-tempered, crotchety, violin-playing father.

Youth

Axel Munthe was enrolled as a student at Uppsala University in 1874 and two years later he took his degree in ' Philosophy of Medicine '.

Neither the borrower's lists in the great library nor other records of the more serious side of university life show any sign of great activity on Axel's part. It seems probable that here again he read only what was absolutely necessary for examinations. Only in the gay record of the students' Union will the biographer be rewarded and then richly, if a little oddly, by many references to the jollities and laughter of years ago with here and there the mark, the same easily recognizable mark, that half-puckish, half-naïve humour which all who ever knew him will remember. In debate he is described as a powerful and attractive speaker, on musical occasions as having a rich warm singing voice, at celebrations, commemorations and parties as invaluable for his gaiety which was all the gayer for being unforced and unsophisticated.

Even in those days he showed no sense of the practical realities of life. He soon became well known for running a small idealistic and vaguely Robin Hood-like state of his own in which he shared what little resources he had with anyone who happened to be in need, regardless of whether the applicant was in any way worthy. At this early stage he seemed already to have a magnetic attraction for the unfortunates of the world. His detractors suggested he liked them as subjects for his studies in human psychology.

His university career was unexpectedly cut short by ill-health. He had never been robust and in spite of his efforts

[17]

to overcome his weakness, a delicacy of the chest developed
and was considered so serious that he was sent to the Riviera
for the winter. He was not expected to live and a friend of
the family who met him in Italy wrote home: " he looks to
me as if he won't last long, soon to go to a happier world ".

This was his first journey to the south; his first sight of
France, the Mediterranean, the wonderful treasures that he was
to love throughout his long life. While recuperating in
Mentone he made the acquaintance of the famous French
gynæcologist, Professor Courty. Courty took a liking to him
and invited him to his laboratories in Montpellier. After a
few months Axel's health had improved sufficiently for him
to decide to accept Courty's offer, and he was enrolled as a
student in the Faculty of Medicine at Montpellier University.

With the flaming enthusiasm typical of his whole nature as
soon as his imagination was roused, he flung himself into the
work; psychology under Professor Rouget and surgery under
the celebrated Dubreuil. The work engrossed him entirely,
he thought of nothing else and his rapid progress was much
commented upon by those who watched him. The following
year, so great was his promise that he was sent to Paris to
complete his studies at the very centre of French medical
learning. There also he worked day and night: he was
absorbed into his natural element, and by August 1880 he was
ready to take his degree as Doctor of Medicine.

His doctor's thesis called *Phrophilaxie et Traitement des
Haemorragie* attracted much attention and the dissertation
which followed is described as causing a ' veritable sensation ',
though unfortunately not in a manner likely to advance the
career of a young unknown beginner. The whole affair
nearly ended in disaster. The candidate had taken his place,
according to custom, on the steps of the professorial ' chair ',
for he could only mount the platform when the dissertation
was over and the time had come to ' harangue ' the assembled

faculty. The presiding professor, who appears not to have viewed very favourably Axel's candidature, made a cutting reply, expressing pained surprise at the temerity of this young foreigner who, while aspiring to enter the close circle of the Parisian mèdical world, should nevertheless persist, throughout his thesis, in quoting mostly non-French medical writers such as Scanzoni or the German Spiegelberg, when everyone knew that the Paris Faculty abounded with illustrious names and mines of information which he could better have quoted.

Axel took every word to heart and was amazed; but worse than that he sought to defend himself. Unable to contain his indignant fury, he leapt on to the sacred rostrum and blurted out: "Messieurs je ne suis pas ici pour chanter vos éloges", and to the delight of the students and younger doctors in the auditorium proceeded to say that he had never been given to understand that international political rivalry should form part of scientific gynæcology, but that he was quite prepared to introduce some such political creed if it could be proved desirable. He must however deplore the fact that the world-famous German doctor he had referred to, and whom he genuinely believed to be the foremost authority in that field, should be virtually unrecognized in the Paris Faculty! Such a lugubrious fact, however, could surely not be expected to make him blind to truth or to render him a willing accessory to some scheme for the exclusive glorification of French scientists, though on the other hand no man could be more ready than himself to praise French greatness where in fact it really existed.

By now, feeling was running high and the additional taunt that Axel had used Latin terms instead of French ones so as to show off his classical education had the unforeseen effect of whipping up the audience still further to demonstrate its sympathy for the Swedish youth who was fighting his lone battle before them. The normal twenty minutes allotted to the customary formality of a dissertation had turned into a two and a half hours' passionate wrangle, but at the end of it, the newest and also the youngest doctor ever to be admitted to the French Faculty was excitedly acclaimed: twenty-two-year-old Doctor Axel Munthe.

Axel's own opinion of his performance appears in a letter dated 8th August 1880—"My thesis, extremely poor in all respects, is attached. The only possible explanation of the ultimate success must be the exams. They went well. But, as I say, the thesis is unclear, half finished and weak. However, when I have time, and the means, I shall turn out something respectable on the same subject."

At this point in his career, almost directly after his first foot-hold in Paris was firmly made, he once again let the southern sun lure him, and Italy, with plans for settling there, is constantly in his mind. A French family had invited him to accompany them on a journey to Italy and Egypt. He writes: "I am thinking of accepting, especially as the idea of applying for the post of doctor at the French Hospital in Rome is growing on me. It really seems a practical possibility! If troubles out East should end in war I could always get out there from Italy as an officer in the Red Cross."

That year, far away in Sweden as the April snows began to melt, his mother, who had long been in delicate health, died. The old home was now empty. Inheritance brought some benefit to the second son and in a letter to the executor Axel writes: " . . . you tell me I have some money to come which I did not expect. I shall at last invest in some of the instruments I badly need. Over here it is not like at home where a couple of knives are all one needs; in Paris every kind of implement is required, to get one anywhere. Even as assistant surgeon I had to buy quite a lot of things, and I am still short of much useful equipment which I might find absolutely essential any day now and which, though very expensive, does not look like getting any cheaper. I think I should do well to buy them out here where I am in touch with the manufacturers and can get favourable prices. I have been practising eye operations and am longing to get a complete set of eye instruments if only I had the means, also gynæcological instruments. Is there any chance of getting an advance on my money so as to buy soon? Naturally I cannot get everything I most need at once, but the more urgent necessities would be covered by about 1000 crowns."

He adds that he would like the money sent to his "friend and chargé d'affaires" a young medical colleague called Thedenius. He also announces that the 500 crowns received the day before have already been swallowed up by the landlady and the printer. This letter seems to have been sympathetically received; the 1000 crowns arrived by return of post.

The following autumn Axel suddenly appeared in Stockholm and shortly afterwards he married on November 24 in Klara Church, set deep in an old square of tall seventeenth-century houses, the nineteen-year-old Ultima Hornberg.

The customary bachelors' party on the eve of the wedding was long remembered in Stockholm, largely because the arrangements were in the hands of Axel's friend Carl Larsson the painter. The room was decorated with cartoons illustrating the life and adventures of the groom, and several of Stockholm's younger poets wrote verses which were sung to popular tunes. The most notable episode dealt with Axel's escapades in Sicily when he explored it with his dog Puck and sought out the infamous robber chief Leone. He had succeeded in finding the robbers, but was kidnapped by them and carried off to their caves on the slopes of Mount Etna. Fortunately for the prisoner this band of pirates had recently been involved in an unhappy combat with the militia and their leader had been captured. Their camp was filled with their wounded and these provided the means of salvation for Axel. He practised his skill upon them and became the trusted medical adviser and friend of the Gunelli brothers who were Leone's adjutants. Axel used to maintain that these men were at heart perfect gentlemen and that they understood the art of living to a high degree, though admittedly they had not yet reached the stage of perfection where they could also understand how to let others live. Sung lustily to Silvas' aria " What a Madman!" from the opera *Ernani*, the verses described conspiracies by moonlight sealed with a brotherly shake of the robber's hand all dripping with fresh human blood—in fact a perfect preparation for a bridegroom!

The marriage lasted eight years. Those who knew the bride describe her as exceptionally captivating. In later years Axel Munthe hardly ever spoke of his first marriage, but on those rare occasions words were bitter. And yet in old age he was often to say of himself, " I was not cut out to be a family man!" The fault in this case probably lay on both sides. After the divorce Ultima Hornberg married an Italian and died while still in her youth in 1895.

The young couple travelled to Capri directly after their marriage and there they remained nearly a year. During this stay a serious typhus epidemic broke out. Axel offered his services free and worked unsparingly. In every cottage, hovel, and mountain shepherd's cave he sought out the sick and dying and stopped with them throughout their misery until the scourge had passed. The islanders never forgot this and the King of Italy awarded him a decoration, the first of these highly coveted medals which were to increase year by year and which, truth to tell, he prized so little, lost so often, and never could find when his friends desired most to show him off.

In March 1881 another opportunity to serve came his way and, as before, he seized it without a moment's doubt. Ischia, the larger island in the bay of Naples, was wrecked and torn by the great earthquake. Hundreds lost homes, limbs, lives, and only the scantiest, tragically insufficient medical aid could be found to help them. Axel went over immediately and, almost single-handed, worked with all the intemperate energy which people were now beginning to expect of him. When autumn came, tired and with exhausted nerves, Axel left Italy with his wife and they made for Paris where he had decided to set up his practice.

Three years were to go by before he heard once more the same urgent call to serve Italy in her misery. These three years were spent busily in Paris. It was then, during a holiday in Lapland, in the peaceful loneliness of the stark mountains, that he came upon a copy of *The Times* left, in the cottage where he was sheltering, by an English traveller who had passed that way some days earlier. A headline read ' Cholera brings disaster to Naples '. Within an hour all his plans were changed, his rucksack was packed and he was on his way. Sixty years later when he sat in the great armchair up in his rooms in the Palace of Stockholm planning, cancelling, re-planning, altering and always postponing the longed-for last journey to his Capri fortress, he murmured as his dejected head sank on his breast, " How easy it was then, Lapland to Naples, across the whole of Europe, with no forethought; and to-day with every modern invention by train, by sea, by air— I shall never get away!"

The ghastly scenes that met him on his arrival in Naples are described in his own words in *The Story of San Michele*. At 28 years old Axel Munthe had seen sights and lived through perils that most people would not meet in a lifetime. His character and personality were already becoming strongly marked and noticeable even to strangers meeting him casually. People meeting him abroad for the first time were already writing home about him. One such letter from a family called Cederlund, father, mother and son, is dated 1885 and is addressed to their daughter in Stockholm.

" We return to Rome tomorrow and then north, so it is about time to introduce to you the cicerone we met on the latter part of our journey, no less a person than Dr. Munthe! . . . You can imagine what a difference it has made to our whole trip. He knows these parts better than we know Stockholm. To attempt to give you a picture of him is as fruitless as trying to picture Capri for you!—it all sounds just as flat! One can only confirm that he is indeed an unusual creature in heart and character. Much more aesthetically developed than most people and yet a thorough child of nature.

" As soon as we set foot on Capri we couldn't help feeling proud to be his compatriots. They all ran to embrace him, old men, old women, young peasants and children; they were all happy because he was back—the rich as well as the poor. He took it all without the slightest personal pride, he very obviously loves them too. It was really impressive and I feel that until one has witnessed one of his returns amongst these people, when they welcome him home from abroad, one cannot fully appreciate those amazing tales in his ' Golfo di Napoli ' book. The reason I have not mentioned our meeting with him until now, is on account of his longing to keep his present visit as far as possible incognito. He was hoping to have a completely quiet holiday here and a long rest to try to recover from the strain and exhaustion he suffered after his work in the cholera plague last year at Naples. However, to judge by the queues of people besieging his door from early morning to late night in the hope he will cure their every illness, I doubt he will find any rest at Capri. They say he cannot possibly live long if he continues as at present."

In the Paris of the eighties, Axel Munthe and his pretty wife played their part in the Swedish colony. He was a favourite with the Swedish envoy and minister, Sibbern, and they were often to be seen at the Legation and amongst the young artists, many of whom were to make great names in the future. Carl

Larsson, Ernst Josephson whom Axel nursed through a long illness and who painted a portrait of the young, half-blind, half-farseeing doctor; Forsberg, Zorn, Prince Eugene Bernadotte and of course his own sister Anna and her husband, were all his friends. Amongst them he met the young painter Hugo Birger who, smitten with incurable tuberculosis, worked on in the gay circle with his lovely Spanish wife while death advanced upon him unseen by any save the doctor. Axel Munthe's letters to Birger's father in Stockholm are included in the biography of the artist by Sixten Strombom. Towards the end Birger himself suddenly understood he was ill and decided, too late, to make a last bid for life. He agreed to go to Arendal sanatorium in Norway. Axel arranged for a friend of his to take charge of Birger once he got there and himself immediately prepared to make the long journey to Norway with the dying painter. Birger's Spanish wife Matilde insisted on coming too. There was no money with which to pay the fares, so Axel provided the necessary funds and the three set off. As they sighted the first rocks of Swedish territory at Halsingborg, Axel perceived that his friend was near his end. From Mollberg's hotel he wrote to Hugo's father, addressing him as was customary from a young man to an older one, "Good Uncle! As Hugo wishes we are stopping here instead of carrying on to Gothenberg. The journey has gone fairly well. Hugo was not too tired, though neither Matilde nor I managed to get a wink of sleep after leaving Paris Thursday. Hugo's condition is deteriorating so rapidly that if the journey was to take place at all it had to be at once. Uncle can understand I feel sure, without any words of mine, that there can be no hope of curing a galloping consumption which is spreading as fast as this one."

Before setting out from Paris, Axel had told the young wife that there could be no hope of saving Hugo. But they kept this knowledge to themselves and throughout this farewell journey Axel did all he could to make his friend's last hours as happy and gay as possible. The night he died, the little company of three had drunk a bottle of champagne in Hugo's hotel bedroom to celebrate their safe arrival in Sweden and had laughed a lot and told stories until late, when the young artist finally lay down to sleep without any fear and without even noticing that Death had only a few more minutes to wait.

Axel Munthe did not desert the old father and the wife. He paid up all outstanding bills and settled the old debts that trailed on afterwards. He arranged for the sale of Hugo's pictures as a benefit for his family and was largely responsible for bringing his works to the notice of the best critics of the day. For years he supported the aged and broken father whose little printing business had been failing for years and was now beyond recovery. He kept an intermittent watch on Matilde, intermittent but still faithful even when he had reached his ninetieth year, as a letter written in a shaky Spanish hand in 1948 testifies, thanking " Mon Chér Docteur " for a large sum of money without which life after the Second World War would have been very hard, in the ravaged French countryside near Pau. When Forsberg the painter started a collection to raise money to repay Munthe, Axel was furious and insisted that each subscriber should have his money back.

The correspondence with Birger's father goes on for years after the son's death. In 1888 he is still worrying over the family and finding the usual suspicions and backbiting from the outside world.

" I have been ill all summer," Axel writes. " I have read with much distress what you tell me about that foolish gossip which now wants to make out that poor Matilde has shared the fate of Countess S. in regard to myself! I can only say that I don't give a damn for what these fools say—but honestly, don't we live in an odd world, where the wages of the helping hand are to be nothing but libel? Yes! indeed! the fate of those who try to help is worse than the fate of the scandal-mongers—but instinctively I prefer the former role." Later he writes, " I am not at all well and if I don't manage to find a cure before this winter I foresee Hugo's end is in store for me. My spirit seems broken, finally; and on top of it all money troubles! I shall not spend the winter in Paris, must try seriously to get back my health first—but where? there again finance is the trouble. I'm ruined and until I have written to gather some more money, I can do nothing!"

This need to abandon Paris and the raw, misty Seine was to cut him off from the picturesque bohemian friends of his earlier years. The only one who was to remain throughout his life, and whom we meet again at the end in the Palace of Stockholm, was the fine old painter prince, brother of King Gustaf V, Eugene of Bernadotte. Prince Eugene died a few months before his old friend and his loss struck hard at Axel Munthe, who had enjoyed the artist's keen imaginative society and had admired his work when both were young. In their old age the prince was still painting and Axel still as glad as ever to admire critically his work and his fine collection of contemporary pictures. When they were failing and sick, towards the end, they could still exchange greetings by tele-gram; short but humorous, transmitted on festively decorated forms for every occasion. Art had been Axel Munthe's inspiration just as music had been his solace all through life.

The musical background had been strong. In Axel's boy-hood, summer holidays or winter evenings were often spent with his cousins at ' Beateberg ', the little eighteenth-century mansion which in those days was looked upon as one of the most prominent centres for the musical life of Stockholm. Axel's great grandfather, the political leader of Gustaf III's days, found it convenient to live during sessions of Parliament on this property just outside the capital by the shores of Lake

Sagsjon. The house was considered to be one of the master-pieces of the fashionable eighteenth-century architect Jean Eric Rehn, and was in due course left to his son the ' Young Master Carl ' of the old song, and he renamed it after his wife, Beata Lovisa Drake of Hagelsrum.

' Beateberg ' with its fine old house, now long since pulled down, was in Axel Munthe's youth one of the most idyllic and exquisite summer retreats near Stockholm. In 1839, after the death of ' Young Master Carl ', it had gone to his cousin Henrik Mathias Munthe who was a quiet, kind-hearted man loved by many friends and much appreciated as a fine amateur violinist. When King Oscar II succeeded to the throne, Henrik Mathias was elected to take his place as President of the Academy of Music. He had a fine voice, was a founder of the Bellman Society in 1824, and was considered to be one of the best singers of Bellman's *lieder* in the country. His two sons who lived on into the 1920's carried on the musical traditions of the family whose greatest claim to musical fame lay, as they proudly used to point out, in their connection with Jenny Lind. Henrik Mathias Munthe was her guardian, fatherly friend and protector. Throughout her career which took the ' Swedish Nightingale ' to every capital in Europe, he looked after her affairs in Sweden and always kept her room ready for her visits home, as for any child of the family. At Beateberg the old mill-house by the water's edge was fitted up for her and here in the summer evenings her golden voice would fall upon the still water. Here, too, stood the famous piano presented by the enraptured Viennese to the great singer in 1854. And it was in these rooms, amongst these people, that Axel first learned to understand music. " Music!" he would say in the last years, when he was no longer able to play on his piano or accompany his own voice—" music was the only thing I really knew something about ".

Before he finally abandoned his Paris practice Axel Munthe

had taken one big step in his career as a doctor. He had gradually but irrevocably become established in the minds not only of his patients but also of his colleagues as a nerve specialist. By the time he drew up his roots from Paris he had given up gynaecology and the research which had been his first interest, and had delved deep into the little known, and in those days much mistrusted, realms of medicine which sought to understand nervous disorders, and madness. Axel had become fascinated by the discoveries of the great Jean-Martin Charcot whose work at the Salpêtrière hospital amongst women suffering from chronic diseases had made him the talk of Paris. Everybody, from elegantly dressed society ladies to earnest students of medicine, flocked to his Tuesday afternoon lectures, drawn by the mysterious problems of hysteria and hypnotism which he ruthlessly examined: and even Guy de Maupassant came to listen, and there he met for the first time Axel Munthe, Charcot's pupil.

Axel's association with Charcot came to a sudden and dramatic end. We are given part of the story in *San Michele*, where he tells us how he tried to save the beautiful peasant girl, Geneviève, from the Salpêtrière. He attempted hypnotism: the experiment failed and the great Master never forgave his pupil. So says Axel Munthe, but whatever the truth of the matter may have been Charcot exerted an influence over his brilliant disciple which was to transform his whole career as a doctor.

Mountains and Animals

ANY ARTICLES BY AXEL MUNTHE APPEARED FROM time to time in Stockholm newspapers, and in the autumn of 1885 the *Aftonblad* described him as their Paris correspondent. He signed himself P. M. for Puck Munthe, the name he had given his dog. The earlier articles dealt entirely with politics, and the radical and unconventional views of the writer are easily recognizable. In November 1885 he wrote about the latest parliamentary elections. He pointed to the increased majority of the parties of the Right in the Chamber of Deputies. With the triumph of General Boulanger the fortunes of the monarchical element were thought to be once again in the ascendant. Puck Munthe, however, did not hesitate to declare his staunch belief in the Republic:

" The parties of the Right should not imagine that their considerable gains represent any change in the attitude of France towards Republicanism. . . . The two hundred and two votes of the Deputies should not be interpreted as sympathy with the Royalist cause. . . . The future of the French Republic is more firmly assured than ever."

Later these articles were followed by a new series on mountaineering in Switzerland. Feeling that he had at last overcome the weakness of his early youth, he longed to try his new-found strength. The immensity of the Alps' towering pinnacles, the deathly silent gorges, attracted strongly his uneven nature. He needed the grandeur of the lonely ice peaks and the peace of the clear air. He wanted to feel the serenity of dawn in the sky and the terror of black clouds

[30]

torn by lightning coursing down the mountain-side. In September 1886 an evening issue of the *Aftonblad* contained his ' Snowstorm '.

It opens with the burial, in the little Anglican chapel at Zermatt, of a young Englishman called Burkhart, who had tried to climb the Matterhorn. The snowstorm had over-taken him. His companion and the guide had called and searched and then gone on to escape the blizzard, leaving him to die alone. " I saw the body. There was no trace of fear or agony on his calm features. He looked like a young man asleep, no last tortured struggle with death had wakened him."

Axel's unequivocal sense of fairness made him champion wholeheartedly the cause of the dead youth's companions who were accused, by an indignant public, of deserting him in his hour of need. " Don't talk about heroism and self-sacrifice; all that can be very fine and right when saving other lives from a sinking ship or suffering one's own death rather than fail a friend. But in this case where death came from cold and exhaustion such heroics don't apply. A gradual numbness creeps over the body and spirit alike, the instinct for self-preservation ceases at an early stage, energy is dead and the mind is no longer active. This human is neither brave nor cowardly now, neither high-minded nor low, his individual characteristics are already snowed over and all that made him different from his fellows belongs to past history. I can think of at least one man who God knows is no better at mountaineering than anything else, but who was unwise enough to imagine himself an expert. He climbed up in cheery foolhardiness to the dizziest heights and then, when by the grace of God he had managed to scramble safely down again, he thought fit to brag about this feat as though it had been child's play for him with his giant strength and long young legs. But he never dared to own up to any man, let alone to himself, that on many a mountain crest he had felt sorry for what his creditors were about to lose. And when in doubtful triumph he had stood upon the tallest peak he scarcely could breathe for fear . . . and then, the game turning into a struggle with death, the picnic party into a panic, he flung the responsibility, the tackle, and himself upon the guide, who, amazed to perceive that all the big talk was false, that all the brave show of strength was nothing but a feverish flicker from a fading flame, had to shoulder this weakling child of civilization who had pretended to be such a paragon, this sinewy man. . . . who could neither walk nor stand alone. . . . It is not Burkhart's portrait I am showing you nor that of other lovers of the Matterhorn, but the picture of a foolish traveller who suddenly developed a mania for finding out if the world above the clouds was nicer than the one below. He went up a bragging Alpine climber and came down a pathetic sight. He set out in fun and came down a more thoughtful man."

In an article dated October 20th of the same year, he tells of his ascent of Mont Blanc, ' Le roi des Montagnes '. The expedition in fact very nearly ended in disaster. Vividly he describes the tremendous bitter cold peaks wrapped in equinoctial storms. " To those who did not share in the little adventure on Mont Blanc my tale may seem like madness, nor can I truthfully offer any sane explanation. I have never claimed to be entirely in my right mind, around midsummer time." But the ascent had been attempted long after midsummer, far too late in the season for safety, and this time Axel's trusty friend Puck, the Alsatian dog, had not been allowed to follow. " He had worn out his boots on the Matterhorn. . . . The storms thundered over our heads as though the mighty roof of the whole heavenly palace were crashing down to hell and at our heels like a famished sleuth hound Bore the Frost god ran after us, in the end overtaking and nipping off my toes. . . . The snow kept opening beneath our shambling feet like a quicksand sucking its victims downwards. The solid-looking white ground gave way and caved in. I felt myself tumbling helplessly down to the nether regions. Then I found myself lying in a bleak and dark blue grotto of silence. The deathly cold was laying hold of me, creeping round my limbs freezing me slowly to death. Suddenly the instinct of self-preservation made its last struggle; I sat up in my ice coffin." Here he quotes for the first time the lines of Heine he was to repeat so often in his last years in Stockholm. " Death is nothing; but dying is shameful."

All his later life he was to suffer from frost bite in one foot, and later that winter Swedish friends who met him in Paris describe him as an invalid, " One foot bound up and a high temperature, all as a result of his mountain climbing, waiting for an operation on his frozen foot but nevertheless as pleased as Punch with his adventure."

His tales from the Alps appeared in various papers and they called forth a long and heated correspondence from other expert and amateur mountaineers. His dog would invariably reply on his behalf in the columns of the Press, signing himself " Puck Munthe, member of the Alpine Club ".

This four-footed Alpinist became involved at one point in an argument about courage: " Compliments for courage displayed are usually just as insecurely founded as taunts at cowardice. Both can only be suspected, guessed at, but no one can say of another man, how much courage he required to meet a certain danger or how much cowardice he showed. I maintain that one can measure the extent of danger in which a particular person finds himself at a given moment by comparing his chances of success with his chances of disaster, but I never maintained that one could use this yard-stick to measure his courage. It is not the peril inherent in the situation which determines the amount of courage required to meet it but the entirely arbitrary and individual assessment of peril by the mind of that particular person, which indicates whether he displayed less or greater courage. . . . Mankind can display many forms of courage. Courage in battle which can sometimes be closely akin to recklessness in a hero devoid of much thought or sensitivity—Tolstoy has made a masterly analysis of this. Courage in religious conviction, which reaches more nearly to ecstasy in its most sublime form, courage in the face of darkness which must be the noblest of all. . . ." At a later stage he says, in another letter, " The finest courage in the original sense of the word is surely that bravery a poor creature manages to show after fear has already entered his heart."

*   *   *

Axel Munthe's long fight to protect the rights of animals was to go on for more than sixty years, but in the end it won its victories. One of these was the creation of a sanctuary on the island of Capri, the half-way resting-place for immense flocks of migratory birds in their journey twice a year between the northern and southern hemispheres.

As a young man he had contributed to Stockholm's *Dagblad* articles which gained him little sympathy. He pitted his strength against the age-old interests of the chase. To frighten, to chase and to kill may be inevitable when mankind must seek food to live upon, but as a mere pastime and sport for civilized man, it seemed to him utterly inexcusable and inhuman.

Later he turned his attack on the cramped and miserable conditions of travelling menageries. With characteristic zeal he defends the powerless pent-up wrath of an old baboon to whom he used to bring an extra lump of sugar after he learned that it had bitten off the thumb of a woman who had poked at it with her umbrella. He apostrophizes the proud nubian lion Brutus, still defiant after its long defeat, " Brutus, Brutus avenger of freedom destroyed, you are too mighty to be a slave! Wrench off the chains in which men's creeping cunning has ensnared the slumbering powers of your world! Shake back your flaming mane and, strong as Samson in your glorious rage, bring down the prison walls upon the gaping Philistines who gather to gloat unfeelingly over their captive's despair." The words of a very young man written on a Christmas Eve.

" The Zoological Gardens where, like a would-be Darwin, one can watch and study the ways and habits of animals, are surely justifiable. So also is vivisection practised by serious scientists. But travelling menageries are not to be tolerated any more than vivisection should be undertaken by dilettantes. The barred cages of the fair-ground have nothing whatever to do with science. They have never contributed to any scientific discovery, they are nothing but houses of cruelty and suffering for every animal trapped within them. . . . The sympathy which stretches a little beyond the affairs of men and women, the pity which extends even to dumb animals, these moral attributes seem to be the last granted to mankind in his slow development. Anyone who wishes to dispute the truth of this statement should refer to Darwin. The attributes of sympathy and pity are never found at all in the less developed races of humanity, and the extent to which a man can suffer on behalf of an animal friend is an excellent measure of the level of civilization to which he has attained. He who baits dumb animals can only be considered as a primitive specimen of man in the transition stage from the savage to the modern human being. He is the missing link between the crude original and the most finely developed type."

But, unlike some animal lovers, Axel Munthe never sank

into useless sentimentality. The extract quoted above about vivisection shows his realistic approach to the whole question. So does the following passage from his description of climbing the Matterhorn; the climber with his dog is Axel and Puck: "I know another person who fared badly on that day when Burkhart died: but coming from the other side as he did he was luckier than the party who set out from Zermatt, even though he would have been still more hopelessly out of reach of rescue if disaster had actually overtaken him. This poor person had a dog, of whom he was very fond and for whom he honestly believed he would give his life if need be. And yet, lo and behold, on that fatal day when the storm was taking its toll of the rash men who braved the raging elements that person was quite ready to cut the rope and leave his four-footed friend in the fast gathering snow. He felt no shame or sorrow at the thought of deserting him, and he had even made up his mind that if the snow were to go on falling for another two hours he would sacrifice his dog. Dog lovers may despise him heartily for this but it cannot be helped—those are the facts." But the faithful Puck of this story followed his master everywhere he went as long as life lasted.

It seems to be quite normal for dogs to be named after humans but not so normal for humans to be named after dogs. All Axel's early writings are signed P. M. and long before his master's name was to become a household word in the world of books, the dog had already become famous. Puck seems to have deserved the honour. Photographs show him with his great heavy head and solemn eyes, an Alsatian with the body of a young lion and muscles of iron. Friends used to say that as a result of sharing his life so completely with Axel Munthe the dog gradually developed an almost human understanding. He came to lose all interest in cats or even his own kind. He was engrossed in his master's

life and would observe and judge with utmost wisdom everyone who came near Axel until he was sure they were reliable
friends.

Munthe's work was in time to affect animals of many kinds
in widely separate parts of the world: from acquiring the
mountain-top of Capri and making it a sanctuary under Italian
law for birds of passage between Greenland and the Forests
of Africa, to buying blankets by the thousand to cover cattle
rendered homeless after the burning of the farms in Finland
by the Russian armies in the bitter winter war of 1939–40.
It did not matter where or how; as long as humans failed to
realize their duty to their fellow creatures on this earth, so long
must he spend what wealth he had in repairing the fault whenever it might come to his notice.

San Michele and the Tower of Materita

MOST OF US HAVE BUILT OUR CASTLES IN THE AIR, places where all that we love best in life is supposed to thrive in airy peace unspoiled by too close touch with the busy daily world; places we long for when we feel most tired or overwhelmed. But how few ever live to see their dreams grow into reality—their castles become habitable—like the two Axel Munthe made at Capri.

From the day he first visited Italy, the young Swedish doctor was to come up against two sharply contrasting aspects of the country. We know now how much real physical fear was bound up with the fascination he felt for cholera-stricken Naples. The conditions in which he worked, the awful size of the overcrowded, diseased, filthy and dying city must have turned many a heart sick with the utter hopelessness of its cause. Even Capri was to appear to him first in all the misery of the epidemic. He first landed on that famous, thousand-year-old pleasure ground, not as a sightseer but as a doctor; young, not very experienced, and equipped mostly with a fund of pity and goodwill towards men. Yet eager for beauty, his eyes, which no power was ever to blind completely, must have kindled a brighter blue that day as they first beheld the turquoise water of the gulf, the classic island rising from its midst, laden with history, scented with clusters of oriental flowers shaded with rich foliage above the cliffs of Capri. To the young northerner this must have seemed payment enough for all the seething horror of the pestilence. The white villages huddling on the cliff tops, the cool grottoes by the lapping water's edge,

rina Grande, Capri

The Tower of Materita, Capri

Torre della Guardia, Capri

San Michele, Capri

The Olive Store, near Castello Barbarossa

Castello Barbarossa

the seeming eternity of all this rich beauty worked their spell upon him. And to the natives of the magic isle, in turn, this young man had come as a heaven-sent saviour in their darkest hour. Here was not a visitor to despoil, but to their mystic minds a patron to worship; all that Capri had was his. In all its long history no stranger ever captured Capri so instantly or held it so completely and so long.

Capri today is no longer what it was on that day seventy years ago when Axel Munthe came. In this age of organized tourist travel Capri too has suffered the new sort of invasion. One hotel after another appears. Exotic villas are always being built by more or less well-known people. But in spite of this, for some reason not easy to discover, the almost magic wonder of the place still survives and is there to be felt by those who care.

Marina Grande has spread out of all recognition, but the fancy villas, though individually horrible, somehow fail to spoil the proportions of the whole. The Faraglioni Rocks still stand on guard in the blue water and the Grotta Azurra remains the wonder it always was in spite of the romance-hunting trippers who attack it with giggles and cameras all through the season. High above the little bay, the towering rock of the Palace of Jovis—from which moody Tiberius ruled his Roman world, and from whose parapets he hurled (so say the Capri guides) young boys who disobeyed his imperial will—still crumbles in the burning sun.

In spite of tourists, advertisements and the vulgar glamour it seems impossible, when there, to steel one's heart against Capri. The colour of it all remains unique, the flowers still grow everywhere on old ruins or modern follies, and over it all, high above the din made by the visitors, anyone who steps aside must hear the beating wings of centuries flown by.

The one and only town square looks like the original model for all Italian opera scenes. All the 'properties' are there: the steps leading up to the baroque church, the town hall, the café, the shop fronts, the chorus dressed in all the motley of a theatrical wardrobe. An old man, complete with gold rings in his ears glittering in the shadow of his sombrero hat looking as if the bluest blood of Corsican piracy flowed in his veins, leans against a wall. Bare-footed fishermen and a stately matron with an immense basket of washing on her head pass from the flowing sunlight of the square into the cool mystery of a dark arcade. Figures in black with sharply lined features and shiny black hair strut around confident in the importance of their office. The tourists themselves seem different here, for where else could one see such a background for the display of an American film party, all painted and dressed up for the 'set', sipping coffee while ragged beggar boys run under their feet picking up their discarded cigarette ends.

But the real inhabitants of Capri are the fishermen. Down with their nets and boats they work hard at the traditional industry of the island. Amongst these were the true friends of Axel Munthe from the beginning to the end. One thing about him they never quite understood—his extraordinary attitude towards animals. Italians are not brutal or unkind: they are probably among the most friendly and peace-loving of peoples. But to their way of thinking domestic animals are a part of their goods and chattels. Pots and pans are carefully looked after while they still have use in them, but when they are worn out they are thrown upon the dust heap. Why on earth should one not be allowed to go on banging away at an old donkey until the last drop of usefulness has been got out of it. Surely it is sheer waste to do otherwise.

Equally incomprehensible was Munthe's opinion of the snaring of little birds in nets while they rested on the island. Quite obviously they were a present from the Almighty to the faithful of Capri just as the rain and sun which ripened the grapes were His gift too. Would it not be madness or the worst form of arrogance to refuse these gifts from God? In any case, why should it be more shameful to snare birds with nets on a mountain-top than to catch fish with nets in the sea? He really did have some very odd ideas, this good patron of theirs. Not that anyone could object if he liked to risk his own neck clambering along precipitous rocks trying to shoot some wretched old horse or dog that might have got stuck on some barren ledge. After all, wasn't it usual and simpler to drive a useless animal over the cliff? That was after all his affair, though it did seem a deplorable waste of his time and talents, especially if he should fall and kill himself. But almost worst of all was his determination to prevent the selling of thrushes and other song birds to the kitchens of the rich. God indeed sent His blessings and His trials fairly mixed!

San Michele, called after the old disused chapel around which the house was built, occupies a small piece of barren ground on what must be one of the most beautiful sites in the world. High up above the sheer slopes of Capri with the straggling village of Anacapri to the south of it, this eagle's nest clings to the volcanic rock, and its white colonnaded windows face the Bay of Naples in an unending gaze.

There is a small cluster of houses of which Axel Munthe also owned the little seventeenth-century summer residence of the Bishops of Sorrento next to San Michele. The gardens are adjacent though separated at one point near the road by a tiny plot of ground he never managed to acquire; and now this plot has been turned to considerable personal profit by a resourceful souvenir dealer. Every conceivable relic and memento of Munthe and his work can now be bought there at high prices by incautious admirers: the rustic peace of Munthe's unpretentious house has been violated here at its very doorstep. But still the door looks strong and the walls high and there is a way up to the house from the sea by which one can still avoid the ugly encroachments, up the zigzag narrow steps of Roman construction, through knee-high flowering myrtle and deep blue lithospermum.

San Michele, behind the white wall with its typical South Italian crenellation, is built on the foundations of a Roman villa. No great architect was called in to design it; no fortune was spent in building an indestructible or imposing mansion. Imposing is the last word one could use in describing Axel Munthe's house. He built it largely himself with the help of an old workman as and when his " ships came in ". When he stumbled on a beautiful piece of antique stone-carving he used it in truly mediaeval fashion in the construction to its best advantage. He never conceived it as a museum, he wanted it as a refuge where he could dream and write in peace; where he could feel and live the natural existence of the men of mediaeval or classical days before the world became so complicated. He abhorred luxury and extravagance; there is none at San Michele. Those who expect a dazzling palace are disappointed. His greatest achievement here was his skill in taking the best advantage of every feature of the site. Who that has wandered under his pergola and leant against the marble twisted columns of the arcade and reached the parapet beyond and touched the red granite haunches of the silent sphinx, set as though gazing for ever at the stupendous vision of blue far below and away into the distant sky—who could deny the imagination that gave to the mysterious stone goddess of Egypt such a fabulous eternal view? But there is no face beneath its granite mane.

Long before San Michele was completed Axel Munthe had taken up his practice in Rome and had his working home in the apartments where Keats and Shelley had lived before him, overlooking the monumental steps of the Piazza di Spagna. From the heat and bustle of Rome he would escape for a few days to continue the building of his castle-in-the-air at San Michele. Years went by as he collected the beautiful old Italian furniture and the carved heads of mediaeval Princes, adding on a room and taking down another, until at last he completed it as it stands today; only to lose the desire to live there any more. The actual building of it had been his pleasure. By the time that it was perfect he had already become famous. His connection with the Court in Sweden brought him still more into the world of fashionable people and even at San Michele they would seek him out. Once the defences of his castle were breached by the people of his everyday life it no longer had any charm for him. He could find no peace there. He and his house had become sights for sightseers.

But a great misfortune befell him about this time. He lost his right eye. The other became inflamed and more and more sensitive to strong light. Each time he came home, the sun, glaring on the white walls of San Michele, smote his sight as he raised his head. San Michele could be of no help to him any more; the last chain that held him had broken and he must go.

On the gentle south-westerly slopes of Capri, where the olives grow best, stands the mediaeval fortress of Materita. Unlike San Michele, arrogantly perched upon its cliff, Materita rests silently amidst the grey shade of the olive trees. It is nearly half an hour's walk along the meandering paths that lead from San Michele down to Materita. The road from romantic youth in all its pride to the lonely resignation of old age. When Axel Munthe made his last home in the old fortress he felt his life to be at an end. In his own words: " As for me the battle is over and lost. I have been driven out of San Michele, the labour of a lifetime. I had built it, stone by stone, with my own hands in the sweat of my brow. I had built it on my knees to be a sanctuary to the sun where

I was to seek knowledge and light from the glorious god I had been worshipping my whole life. I have been warned over and over again by the fire in my eyes that I was not worthy to live there, that my place was in the shade, but I had paid no heed to the warnings. Like the horses returning to their burning stables to perish in the flames, I had come back, summer after summer, to the blinding light of San Michele. Beware of the light, beware of the light!

"I have accepted my fate at last. I am too old to fight a god. I have retreated to my stronghold in the old tower where I mean to make a last stand. Dante was still alive when the monks set to work to build the Tower of Materita, half monastery, half fortress, strong as the rock it stands upon. How often has not his bitter cry of: 'Nessun maggior dolore che ricordarsi del tempo felice nella miseria' echoed through its walls since I came here. But was he right after all, the Florentine seer? Is it true that there is no greater suffering than to remember our past happiness in our misery? I for one do not think so. It is with joy and not with sorrow that my thoughts go back to San Michele, where I have lived the happiest years of my life. But it is true I do not like to go there myself any more—I feel as if I were intruding upon sacred ground, sacred to a past which can never return, when the world was young and the sun was my friend."

But the past was to return, during his 'last stand', and was to carry his name to the farthest corners of the earth. He was old, tired and nearly blind; he was struggling against bitter melancholy, but he was yet to write *The Story of San Michele*.

Torre di Materita is well off the beaten track. Tourists seldom roam so far. It lies low down, no great distance from the sea. Oak trees and olives shade its old walls and from its ramparts there is only one view beyond the grey-green treetops—the wide-open sea, limitless and bleak.

Unlike San Michele, its windows do not look out on Ischia, Vesuvius or Naples, all encircled in the most beautiful bay in the world. Materita faces west. No longer the young rays of the morning sun glittering over the water: instead, at the end of each day, flooding the horizon with blood, the sun sinks in an immensity of sea.

Here in this fortress of the old Kings of Naples he built himself a home which was to become a good deal more habitable than San Michele had ever been, though by no means comfortable according to modern tastes. His bed-room on the first floor can only be reached by a spiral staircase so narrow that a fully grown person has difficulty in getting up. His workroom down below, with massive dark walnut renaissance furniture, is filled with objects he had collected, the things he loved. Fragments of marble, bronzes, old paintings are littered everywhere. Nearly all are antiquities from Capri, Rome, Greece or Egypt, works of art made in the days of the great renaissance. When he admired an unobtainable treasure in some museum and could get a good copy he did not hesitate to place it there, amongst his own originals, as a daily reminder. Only one modern painting in the whole room—his sister Anna's miniature of their father's grandfather, the legendary hero of the Swedish folk-song. There he hangs in scarlet coat and periwig next to Perugino's original portrait of Raphael.

Even as a youth Axel Munthe suffered from bad eyesight. The portrait of him at the age of twenty-two by Ernst Joseph-son, now in Prince Eugene's collection, shows him wearing thick-lensed glasses. His handwriting throughout the years shows the rapid deterioration of his sight. At fifty he was threatened with complete blindness and only by a stroke of luck avoided the loss of both his eyes. During the First World War he managed to serve as a doctor with the Red Cross at the front, but from then on his sight grew steadily worse. In an undated letter to his brother written some time in the 1920's he thanks him for sending his latest book: " But the trouble is that I can only read about two lines at a time and sometimes not even that; soon I shall not be able to read at all. I have no one here who can read Swedish except A's sister and she is a fussy sort of person continually going to bed with some real or imaginary complaint—mostly imaginary—so I shall have to wait until the Queen comes down here and get her or Countess Taube to read it aloud to me. I was quite successful in reading your letter this morning, thanks to the large clear writing. I believe I have a chance of avoiding total blindness for a while at any rate. On the other hand, it may come at any moment. I lost the sight of my right eye in a day. Nothing to be done. Resign myself to my fate. I seem to be able to bear my cross fairly respectably provided I live alone."

The circumstances in which he lost his sight and in part regained it are told elsewhere in this book. Later when it was considered possible to improve the sight of his remaining eye by a further small operation, Axel refused: he preferred to leave well alone. For the remaining years of his life he was able to read a little and could, with his back to the light, at any rate recognize his visitors.

At times he would say he wished he had never had the last operation, he preferred his total blindness. Many unpleasant things, he said, had passed by him unseen and it was much easier to concentrate his thoughts on things that mattered. But sometimes his words belied his meaning.

In *The Story of San Michele* Axel Munthe tells how he learned to use a typewriter when his sight failed him. His fingers were able to find their way about a keyboard without the help of his eyes, when they could no longer write a free-hand letter. But his typing was not easy to read: he seemed largely to trust to luck and to bang away at keys often other than those at which he aimed, which gave his letters a very peculiar appearance.

It was in this way that, with the help of an old Corona machine, *The Story of San Michele* was finally written in 1928.

In 1948 I had to travel to Italy on my own business.

" Will you do me a service as you are going there in any case?" he asked.

" Of course!"

" Bring back my old typewriter; it is on the table in my writing room at Materita."

He was already very weak then and his stiff, tired old fingers were refusing to wield a pen. Once again he imagined the typewriter might work its magic as it had done when he was blind. He fumbled for a piece of paper and painfully scrawled some lines to a friend at Capri—the handwriting is remarkably firm. He began it in English but gradually it turned into Swedish.

As I got nearer to his island I was amazed to find how people still anxiously awaited his return and how eager they were for news of him. Already at Naples the fact of my bearing his name started a queue of Press interviewers. On landing at Capri itself I was besieged by enquiries: when was he coming home? His name seemed to pave the way of my progress.

The old typewriter was discovered and handed over to me with a bunch of rosemary from the walls of the crumbling tower as a greeting from his old housekeeper and her family, Vittorio and Maria, while Lupa, Axel Munthe's last Alsatian dog, sniffed around with evident misgivings.

When I got back to Stockholm and brought my trophy to Axel Munthe I understood at once that it was too late. He would never use it again. He too seemed to understand. "Yes, yes, very good! Put it over there in the corner." He did not even open it.

The Queen's Physician

AXEL MUNTHE'S LIFE WAS DESTINED TO BE FULL OF paradoxes. He who in early youth had held unconventional and radical views was in the end to work and live more than most men in the circle of royalty and Court etiquette. Inadvertently almost, the young volunteer doctor of the poor in Naples was to be landed with a rich clientèle of society beauties on his otherwise occupied hands. To the mind of this nervy, overworked philanthropist the request that he should become Physician-in-Ordinary to Her Royal Highness the Crown Princess Victoria of Sweden came as another call for help rather than as a coveted prize. He seems to have made a spirited effort to free himself from the onerous honour and all the conventional entanglements he could foresee following in its wake. He finally agreed, however, on certain conditions, one of which was that Her Royal Highness should consent to be treated like any other of his less-exalted patients.

This fiction was soon found to be untenable, especially after the Crown Princess became Queen of Sweden. But Axel Munthe persisted in dodging what he considered to be the chains of Court life. He undoubtedly took an impish delight in playing havoc with Palace formalities whenever possible, and scandalizing the more formal-minded courtiers. He became the Court *enfant terrible* and he antagonized many who felt offended by his unconventional behaviour. On the whole the courtiers tolerated this incomprehensible personage because there was in fact no alternative course. Some, on the other hand, looked beyond the peculiarities on the surface and

[48]

let themselves be wholeheartedly captivated by the strong charm of his unusual personality. Among these he made his most lasting friends.

Axel Munthe's new appointment was to bring close together two strong-willed characters. At the time, many who knew them both prophesied an early end to this arrangement. The reverse however was to happen. The exalted patient and her adviser formed a respect for one another which soon turned to trust and understanding, and ended in a warm, lifelong friendship. In his last years, whenever Axel Munthe could be brought to talk of the Queen of Sweden, he plainly showed his deep admiration for her. To him she was a woman of spirit who, undaunted by the outer circumstances which constrained her, adhered throughout her life to her high ideals and crystal clear-cut beliefs. He found in her too a person with many similar tastes—a lover of nature and of all the ancient glories of the southern island where both were to make their second homes. Most of all he appreciated her love of animals. In his early work for the protection of animals Axel Munthe had met very little sympathy and much strong opposition: but from the Queen he was to get never-failing support. When, with Her Majesty's permission, he dedicated to her the first edition of *The Story of San Michele*, he wrote on the first page, not without humour, perhaps, but certainly with sincere feeling: " To Her Majesty Queen Victoria of Sweden, Protectress of Oppressed Animals, and Friend of All Dogs ". The day before her death she made him promise to let that dedication stand in all later editions of his book in Swedish.

That this happy friendship should grow through the long years with never a cloud would be impossible with two such natures. Yet the only long-lasting disagreement, which led to a temporary rift, was caused by the First World War in 1914. Though the decision was difficult and painful, Axel Munthe, who by then had married in England and made a home there, wholeheartedly embraced the allied cause and instantly applied to serve as a doctor at the front. The Queen of Sweden, descended as she was from the ancient Swedish Royal House of Vasa on one side and from the German Grand Dukes of Baden on her father's side, sympathized deeply with the German cause. Munthe handed in his resignation from Her Majesty's Court and immediately sought naturalization as a British subject. He felt convinced that all the Queen's influence would be directed towards pressing Sweden into the war on Germany's side.

The resignation appears never to have been formally accepted, and soon after the war ended he was again the Queen's doctor. But it was not until ten years later that he accepted any salary for his services. There is a letter in which he complains of his financial difficulties at this time due to the expenses of his life at Court and journeys backwards and forwards without any official pay. In another letter, written from Materita on the 14th of September 1929, he finally agrees to be paid: " I gratefully accept the proposal after long reflection, but on the condition that my pay should not come from Her Majesty's private income."

In the distant solitude of their two Anacapri mountain retreats they were able to enjoy each other's society without the irksome formalities of the strict Court etiquette in Sweden, to which the Queen must have found it difficult to make Axel Munthe conform. The story is told how she battled against his obstinate refusal to wear Court uniform and at length succeeded in making him do so by assuring him that the uniform in question had been designed by no less a person than Carl von Linnaeus, the great eighteenth-century botanist who gave to flowers and plants the Latin names still used throughout Europe. She knew well that Munthe was interested in the great Linnaeus, and eagerly watched the effect of her words. Munthe was completely taken in and agreed to order a uniform. However, soon after it was made he discovered the joke and never again did he put on the gaudy attire. The many gorgeous decorations which were lavishly showered upon him from most of the Courts in Europe he treated with a frivolous nonchalance. One day when the organizers of a shooting competition at Capri approached him in the hope that he might care to present some prizes, he considered for a moment, then eagerly plunged his hand into a drawerful of glittering medals and orders and, grinning broadly, handed them to his astonished visitor. On another occasion, when the notorious Field-Marshal Goering visited Capri after a conference with Mussolini and descended upon Axel Munthe's home, the old doctor kept the almighty collaborator of Hitler waiting while he ransacked his drawers with fumbling hands and unseeing eyes for the only decoration he cared about, the French scarlet bouton de la Legion d'Honneur. With this symbol of his last war effort proudly sticking in the buttonhole of his shabby old coat he blindly staggered into the Field-Marshal's gaze.

But the Queen of Sweden did not share his views on decorations and etiquette in general. She was at times apt to misinterpret his attitude as an affront towards herself. Once, on the occasion of an important banquet in Stockholm Palace, the Queen, remembering his weakness, sent her Chamberlain to him with a special request and reminder that he should appear with decorations, "at any rate with the Grand Cross of the Order of the Nordstjarna". Feeling very properly that this time something must be done about it, but having as usual no idea where his decorations were, Axel Munthe hastily sent a message round certain of the Court gentlemen asking if anyone would lend him the insignia for the evening. The Grand Cross of the Nordstjarna arrived at his rooms in good time and was duly pinned on him and royal approval was vouchsafed during the splendid soirée that followed. Not until sometime afterwards was the unfortunate discovery made that the Nordstjarna was one of the orders that had not yet been bestowed upon him! The consternation quickly subsided, no doubt, but the episode provided him with grist for his mill ever afterwards, and never again could he be persuaded to take his decorations seriously, not even when, some years later, he was in fact honoured with the Order of the Nordstjarna.

Axel Munthe held no very exalted opinion about his own ability as a doctor. In fact he had very little respect for doctors in general. The quality which marked him out from his contemporaries was the almost hypnotic will-power which enabled him, more or less subconsciously, to force his patients to do what he wanted. It has been widely acknowledged that it was this power which kept the Queen alive long after she would otherwise have given up the struggle.

Throughout his career as a man of medicine he was to prove, time and again, that after experience and knowledge had been exhausted there was still a power in man which could be called upon to work wonders. There is no doubt now that Axel Munthe possessed this power to an unusual degree.

When in 1925 the Queen accompanied the King on a long and tiring progress through Sweden, ending up with a State visit to Finland, her health was already on the decline. From then on, it steadily grew worse until she was obliged to spend most of the remaining years of her life abroad in southern climates. She returned to Stockholm in 1928 for the Jubilee in connection with King Gustaf V's seventieth birthday. In her longing to spend at least the summers in her beloved Sweden, she travelled laboriously and slowly from Capri, Rome, or Mainau, the eighteenth-century palace on Lake Constance which she had inherited from her parents, to the Royal Palaces in Sweden; a sick lady accompanied by all the retinue and complicated paraphernalia that surround a Queen.

A difficult patient

Amongst the men and women who faithfully played their part in these ponderous last moves, invariably there would appear, a little apart, the gaunt groping figure of Axel Munthe.

Letters, some of them very frank, to the Lord Chamberlain, Printzsköld, describe the downward progress of her long illness. In the spring of 1927 he writes from Anacapri: " . . . the Queen had a bad attack of influenza, both lungs badly affected . . . Nerves in a miserable state . . . The patient was rather difficult to deal with in the beginning of this illness but in the end she obeyed. I have now left her in good shape, at any rate for the time being. I shall return as soon as the irritation in my eye has diminished. . . . As you know we leave Rome on the 15th May. I shall see Her Majesty safely to Mainau. Her brother [the Prince Max of Baden] sounds to me seriously ill, quite apart from his fast approaching blindness. . . . I wrote you from Rome about next winter. It will not be easy to find the right kind of house but I will do what I can. As to the future, I believe, if further mistakes such as were made last summer can be avoided, the Queen will live. Very likely longer than you or I. . . ."

From Mainau he writes on August 20: " . . . the Queen cannot be said to have benefited by her stay here, but on the other hand she is no worse, so on the whole we can feel satisfied. I stick to my belief . . . that she can live several years longer. The influenza this spring was a bad setback, more serious than my bulletins made out—especially as the patient herself was convinced she was dying, which did not make my work easier. . . ."

It was decided to find Her Majesty a residence in Rome for the winter, and after interminable negotiations Munthe arranged for the purchase of Baroness Aliotti's house which was finally to be renamed Villa Svezia. " . . . I hope that M. [Adolf Murray, Marshal of the Royal Household] has explained clearly the position in regard to the house in Rome. If the contract had been completed now it would have been much more difficult to supervise the alterations. Baroness Aliotti asked for 500,000 lire in advance, and demanded that the cost of rebuilding should be borne by the purchaser. Under the present arrangements she herself pays for the rebuilding which is much more satisfactory. The contract is to be signed only after the Legation have inspected and found all in order. There is no danger of the Baroness suddenly breaking the agreement as the drastic replanning of the whole house makes it utterly unfit for any other occupant. The purchase money, at the special request of Baroness Aliotti, is to be paid in Swedish currency, in Stockholm. She intends to invest it in America and thinks it easier so, much easier in any case from the purchaser's point of view. . . ."

A little later he tries again to push the matter on to some conclusion. . . . " My dear friend, I beg you to read through the long letter I have today written to the King, get a decision and then send me a reply by telegram. The question amounts to this: is the Queen to spend next winter in Rome or not? If that is agreed, then I think there is not the slightest doubt you should make up your minds to buy the house. Better terms are out of the question. As you know, the Rome idea did not originate with me, I still remain neutral, but I can assure you that if the Queen is to spend the winters here, this opportunity is the best we are likely to get. The Queen herself is very much in favour. The cost of renting furniture and house, 250,000 lire, seems to me high, but I can get it no lower. To rent unfurnished would be dearer than buying. If it is decided to buy you must discuss it with Beck-Friis; I don't understand that part of it. My job is to make the necessary replanning of the house, which I do understand. [Signed] Your friend Munthe."

The following summer during the Queen's visit to Sweden

her condition became more serious. " . . . As you probably know Her Majesty has been suffering acutely over a prolonged period from stones in the kidney. This has resulted in a considerable loss of strength and courage. . . ."

As the year advanced into autumn the Queen returned to her villa in Rome, but no improvement came. On the 2nd of November Axel Munthe wrote to the Lord Chamberlain: " The King telegraphed me yesterday saying he ' begins to feel uneasy ' in regard to Her Majesty's condition. I have replied that the Queen's strength and courage have slightly improved since her arrival here, but that the recurring attacks of cramp give ground for serious uneasiness. . . ."

The German heart specialist, Krehl, was now summoned. " . . . Krehl and I agree entirely as to the nature and treatment of the attacks but I consider them more serious than he does. They are definitely dangerous as I have already often said. In his letter to the King, Krehl has suggested that His Majesty should urge the Queen, when he writes, to walk much more than she does at present. But I have written to explain to His Majesty that this is not possible, she must not be forced to walk more that she has done recently. It is amazing to me that Krehl should not understand this. . . . Also I have not concealed from the King the fact that I am more pessimistic than Krehl about these attacks which are serious and might easily become fatal. True, they are not due to organic heart disease but to sporadic cramp. This cramp is of a serious kind. Her Majesty arrived here in a deplorable state but she says herself she feels better and I have even succeeded in getting her to lie out on the balcony for an hour or two each day after untold opposition. When she came she was coughing blood. The inflammation of the mucus is worse since the summer but she eats and sleeps well, pulse and temperature are all right and morale good. She is quite happy here as long as she is left in peace and, apart from these attacks of suffocation, I see no immediate danger, though obviously we must face the fact now that the tide is ebbing fast. My position is not easy as you may imagine. Of course she does obey me, but with Krehl she does exactly as she likes; he cannot ever forget that she is a Queen. . . . Everything seems to be going well in the household and everyone is happy. The whole burden seems to fall on me, and I am ill myself but cannot of course leave the sinking ship."

A further cause for worry was the intense annoyance the Queen felt when Princess Marie, former wife of her youngest son Prince Wilhelm, published her memoirs in a popular weekly magazine in Sweden. " . . . I hope Her Majesty's misgivings about possible indiscretions are unfounded, but the fact is that Her Majesty is extremely disturbed about it all. . . . The Queen relies on you to do all that can be done in the matter. I find her worse than when I left her in Baden and do not feel happy about the future."

On the 18th of March he writes a further letter to the Lord Chamberlain from which it appears that his eye trouble is increasing. " My dear friend, The Queen is somewhat quieter since your last letter but still worries about the memoirs. During the past month, in spite of the cold weather, she seems a little better. This last week she has been out every day. For more than a year I have had barely a single day away from my patient and I am now so tired and unable to sleep at nights that I have insisted on Krehl coming to relieve me. I must get some rest. My eyesight grows worse and worse. . . . At Villa Svezia all goes well and they all seem happy enough. The Grand Duchess Hilde is gay and amusing, much to the annoyance and disgust of the Queen. . . ."

June came and Munthe retreated to his home. The Queen once again moved her Court to Mainau, where she lingered until October amongst the memories of her childhood. By November 1928 Munthe's eye had become so much worse that he gave up writing by hand and relied entirely on the antiquated Corona machine with which he was slowly typing out his book. The machine lacked the accents necessary for the Swedish language so he took to writing all his letters in English.

" . . . The patient has gone downhill a good deal since she left here in early June. It is a sinking ship, the question is only how long she can keep afloat. Mentally speaking the Queen is as active as before . . . but she is much weaker. . . . A grave mistake has been committed in Mainau by allowing her to remain in bed the whole time, now more than five months. She ought to have been forced out of bed, she could quite well sit up in a chair as she was wont to do, but both Krehl and Krieg are quite helpless. She does with them what she likes. They are too German to stand up to her. Now it will be very difficult, may even be impossible, to get her out of bed. And never a breath of fresh air in her room. . . . What I fear most is complications from the kidneys. If this does not occur, and we escape influenza, I think anyhow that she may pass the winter . . . and get her out of bed now and then. To get her out of doors is, for the present at least, out of the question. Also to make her walk—she cannot and should not walk— might kill her outright. I am now arranging her own writing-room as a day bedroom and mean to have her carried there if possible every morning. It is of utmost importance that she gets some fresh air. . . . I am getting blinder and blinder, and you can well imagine what this life means to me, but there is nothing to be done but groan and bear it to the bitter end. . . ."

The bitter end came, as he had foretold, after she had passed the winter, in Rome, on the 4th of April 1930.

The long struggle which thus ended had had its effect upon the two men who had followed its course so closely—the King of Sweden and Axel Munthe: their friendship was to grow stronger as the years passed and their contemporaries departed one by one, until the two old gentlemen remained almost alone sharing their memories.

Often they lunched together: and once, while I was sitting in Axel's room in the Palace chatting, he suddenly remembered that it was time to get ready. He called his factotum Vittorio and began laboriously changing into his best coat.

"It's an awful business lunching with the King. It's so dull."

"What does the King think about it then?"

"He also thinks it is dull."

"Then why do you go on meeting for lunch?"

He paused for a moment with one tired arm stuck half in the sleeve of the jacket and seemed to give careful consideration to the question, then muttered mostly to himself: "Well, you see it's more fun being dull together."

The King never failed to show an almost touching concern for his old friend, and took his full share of worry, expectancy and fear in the never-ending game of Axel Munthe's possible journey back to Italy. Time and again I would have to make fresh enquiries about possible routes and modes of travel, and when at last I gave him the details of the latest proposals, he would make the same reply: "I'll ask the King what he thinks about it." The King usually took the view that he had better give up the journey. "You are much better here," he used to say. No doubt his arguments were sound.

After the end of hostilities in 1945, the King planned to visit his favourite Nice once again and, knowing that his old friend still hankered after the south, he offered to take Axel Munthe with him. Much discussion and activity followed but, as before, the whole scheme melted into thin air. Munthe wavered in a sea of indecision and at last suddenly made up his mind to abandon the project. He was too old, he said, to face the many exertions that would be expected of him on such a journey.

Of course there were times when he did not always see eye to eye with his Royal friend and patron, especially during the still autumn days when the forests of Sweden would be invaded by guns and elk stalking. One day when he was more grumpy than usual I asked him what was troubling him this time. After a while the real reason came out. "They can talk of nothing else but killing animals."

But with the Crown Prince, that diligent patron of the arts, there was always a safe subject of conversation in those later years—how to secure the future of San Michele. The idea of making it into a centre for Swedish students of the classic arts who might be in need of a retreat where they could live free from financial worries while completing their studies or writing their theses had gradually been taking shape in his mind. Against this, his original and more conventional intention of leaving it to his eldest son Peter gnawed at his conscience. But in the end the changed conditions after the Second World War became apparent to him. Peter, a promising young artist invalided out of the Forces, stricken with malaria after five war-wasted years, trying to piece together his life as a painter, working mostly in London—how was he to maintain this additional, distant home in the world as it had become? He decided to give it away and, with the patient help of the Crown Prince Gustaf Adolf, the plan took shape—and San Michele became Axel Munthe's last donation.

But of all his friends among the members of the Swedish Royal Family—one seemed bound to Axel Munthe with very special ties. Prince Eugene Bernadotte, the artist brother of the King, whom Axel had known in the Paris of the 'eighties. Now again, the two would often call upon each other and sit for hours talking—remembering the early days of burning youth and fiery actions, the two rebels against rigid convention, now to the world grown old, but to themselves no doubt unchanged. This friend too was to leave him and Axel

Munthe took his death deeply to heart. When the dead Prince was laid in state upon the catafalque hundreds of citizens trooped by to pay their last respects, and one evening they saw an aged gentleman come tottering up, a darkened glass over one eye, flowers in hand, to bid his last farewell.

Few of the old grandees of Axel's day now remained. Yet another was to leave him with a sadder heart when Adolf Murray, Marshal of the King's Palace, died in 1947. Finally there remained the Baron Jean-Jacques de Geer, Chamberlain of the late Queen and trusty friend of Axel Munthe throughout the years. A youngster of 85, he was to survive him.

And yet he did gather new friends right up to the end, and, true to his nature, he picked them with utter disregard for their social standing. His likes and dislikes were usually formed on the spur of an impulse; the first impression was usually irrevocable, but that had always been his way. One of the last friends he collected was one of the palace electricians, who, in his spare time, painted pictures in the vast kitchen of a suite of apartments then unoccupied, but which he had improvised as a studio. Axel Munthe would wander through acres of passages and rooms, unlocking and locking a succession of doors with a bunch of keys attached to his waist by a silver chain, and finally emerge into the secret studio to examine the latest production. If he liked it he would discuss its price and make a purchase: perhaps it was a reminder of his earlier wanderings through tortuous old streets in Italy, ever on the alert for a work of art.

Civis Britannicus

IN 1907, NEARLY A QUARTER OF A CENTURY AFTER HIS FIRST unsuccessful marriage, Axel Munthe married again.

The society in which he then moved, whether in Paris, Rome or London, was at its height of pre-war splendour and he was to see his future wife for the first time at a ball in Rome, the most beautiful girl in the glittering room as he thought—like a Greek statue come to life. They never spoke, nor did he ever forget the sight, till by chance he met her again. She was Hilda, the only daughter of John Pennington Mellor of Beeston. Heir, through his mother, to some of the treasures to which he later added his own collection, Pennington Mellor also owned the Chateau de Françon in the Pyrenees, and here his daughter was born and spent much of her early childhood. Hilda, when she grew up, accompanied her parents in their constant travels between the capitals of Europe: to Paris, where they had a home, they would go in early spring with visits to the Louvre and Versailles; back to England for the summer; to Munich perhaps for the Wagner Festival; and then on to Athens in the autumn or to Rome to look at the wonders of the Renaissance and the classical art. So little by little this girl had learned to love all the beauties which Axel valued most. When they met they discovered that they had in common a world ageless compared to the brittle, exquisite society in which they moved, and which at heart bored them both equally. Since their world was ageless, they did not notice the unusual difference of years between the man of middle age and the girl in her youth. In vain her father and mother protested. In vain they travelled on to change her thoughts. For years they seem to have tried, fondly, to break this attachment, but they failed. On the 16th of May 1907, in London, from No. 17 Hyde Park Terrace, the house of her uncle Frederick Pennington, M.P. for Stockport, Munthe took his bride. In a plain white dress, she married him in the parish church, quietly, true to their own taste, and then away they went to Denmark and Sweden to see wonders that were new to her.

He took her to Leksand, the old wooden village on Lake Siljan in Sweden where, in the simple, white square manor house, they planned to make their home. In the end he was to live there little enough, but to her it remained their home, and year after year she returned, bringing in course of time their two children for happy summer holidays.

When the honeymoon was over Axel and his wife returned to England. They lived in the old bow-fronted house at 31 St. James's Place, Piccadilly, which belonged to Hilda's aunt, Ursula Bright, wife of the famous Liberal statesman, and there in a room overlooking Green Park Axel's two sons were born.

By this marriage, no doubt, Munthe hoped to strengthen further the bonds which already tied him to England. Many of his oldest friends were Englishmen whom, like Lord Dufferin and Ava, he had met during his first years in Rome. Even in the early Paris days he had preferred to write in English, and gradually he was to come to look upon England as another home.

At the beginning of the First World War he served with a British unit of the Red Cross in France. At Materita today, his Sam Browne belt and officer's cap still hang on the peg where he discarded them on his sorrowful return, half blind, destined to spend the remaining months of the war writing the bitter pages of *Red Cross and Iron Cross*. He wrote in English and he must have voiced the feelings of all England.

Gorm

Charcot

From a pastel by Countess Feo Gleichen

Reading his book again now, one notices a sinister similarity between his words written then, and the retribution meted out to the Nazi monsters at Nuremberg by the Allies of 1946. " . . . The day of reckoning will come. The day when the civilized world sets to work to pick out the criminals from the barbarians, the criminals responsible for the atrocities and infamies committed by the savage foe. The documents for the accusation furnished by the accused themselves—a most valuable contribution to the sombre study of German criminology—establish beyond doubt that it is on the leaders and not on the men that the heaviest responsibility will fall. The hanging evidence against several of the commanding German Generals in Belgium is overwhelming—their proclamations to their victims and their orders to their troops contain damning proofs that they are morally and legally responsible for the slaughter of hundreds of helpless civilians, men, women and children."

The book is in the form of fiction, but the " Dr. Martin " is clearly the author himself, with his unshakable, and at times sentimental, belief in England's cause. " Strike hard, Tommy, strike your hardest! It is the salvation of the world you are fighting for! I have known it ever since I was a boy and began to read the history of England! I have known it all along that you were coming. I have known it all along, but God bless you all the same, Tommy, for coming! And God be thanked that you came!"

Although his whole nature rebelled against the German outlook and system of government, he managed to avoid fanaticism. There is an almost classic ring about his words: " Suffering has no nationality and death wears no uniform. . . ." Sometimes during the Second World War he would recall his experiences in the first: " . . . I succeeded so rarely in helping the wounded to live, but at times I was successful in helping them to die."

The German prisoners who were dying would also get words of comfort in good German, the only way he knew how to help them on their unknown journey. As long as there was any hope of saving life Axel Munthe would strain every nerve to keep awake the will to live. But when no hope existed he never hesitated—and latterly he admitted this frankly enough—to use his art to shorten the remaining moments of agony as best he could. His doctor colleagues, who knew his unconventional views on this much disputed subject, would call him to their hopelessly suffering patients to do for them what they themselves did not dare to do.

Munthe's gift for psychology was to stand him in good stead behind the front lines. In *Red Cross and Iron Cross* the little nurse says to the doctor, " ' I know so little, I can barely read and write and you know so much, you know everything. Sister Philippine says that you even know what one thinks!'

" ' Yes, Josephine, now and then I do know what one thinks,' said the doctor with a smile."

That war was to leave Capri untouched, though many, worn in body and spirit, were to find refreshment at San Michele where the Red Cross established a rest house.

It was another Englishman who showed Munthe the way to fresh fields of beauty hitherto unknown to him. Lord Carnarvon, who had long financed the excavations in the Valley of the Kings, in Egypt, was not only a lover of art but also a highly skilled archaeologist and the trusted friend and collaborator of Howard Carter the Egyptologist. Axel Munthe was known to both, and after they had made their amazing discovery of the tomb of Tutenkamen, they invited Dr. Munthe to assist them at the opening of the coffin. Expectations had been raised to a high level by the gradual unearthing of surrounding graves and outer chambers of the tomb, filled with precious ornaments and costly furniture inlaid with beaten gold and wondrous enamels and jewels.

Before sailing to join his friends, Axel Munthe wrote to his brother in December, 1923. " . . . Tomorrow I leave for Luxor to spend a month with Carter who discovered Tutenkamen's grave. I may have lost interest in most things now, but I still find a fascination in the marvellous artistry of the old Egyptians." So Axel Munthe was to be one of the five persons who witnessed the final unsealing of the innermost coffin, and the uncovering, after more than 3,000 years, of the dead Pharaoh. These five alone were to behold the royal youth in all his original beauty and magnificence, before the body crumbled away under their gaze.

This amazing sight made a deep impression on Munthe's sensitive imagination, and ever afterwards he used to return to those memories as though drawn by the spells of that lost civilization. Lord Carnarvon died soon after the excavation of the tomb, and though the cause of his death was accepted by Munthe as being due to infection following a poisonous mosquito bite, many fanciful minds quickly began to conjure with the old sayings about the curse of the mummy. And even when Howard Carter died, years later in England, at a ripe old age, the same eager seekers after sensation would mutter about the eternal curse. And when, nearing his ninetieth birthday, Munthe still heard the ghost hunters talking of the curse of the mummy in his presence he would say: " Then the curse must have fallen on me too, but in reverse, they have let me outlive myself and even death is not allowed to help me." But who could tell when he was joking or in earnest? He had always suffered from an innate pessimism. On his left hand he used to wear a massive Egyptian ring of bright yellow gold in the shape of a double-headed serpent, Pharaoh's badge, signifying Upper and Lower Egypt. Some months before his death he took it off and laid it aside in his dressing-case. The night before he died he asked for it to be put on his finger. That night was one of torment for him. When the dawn came it slipped from his finger for the last time. Some hours later he died.

The Doctor *

FIRST IMPRESSION

Iᴛ ᴡᴀs ᴍᴀɴʏ ʏᴇᴀʀs ᴀɢᴏ: ᴡᴇ ᴋɴᴇᴡ Axᴇʟ Mᴜɴᴛʜᴇ ᴏɴʟʏ
from hearsay as the author of a small work, long out of
print, which described the cholera epidemic in Naples, and
was called *Letters from a Mourning City*. They were reports
which the author had sent to a Swedish newspaper and which
had subsequently been put together in an English translation.

We had all read the book in turn. The author wrote under
the name of ' Puck Munthe ', and that was all we knew about
him. Puck was his enormous dog, who was with him during
all his Neapolitan adventures.

I was on my first visit to Capri. It was spring; rambler-roses
and wistaria were in full bloom, and during the warm nights
one heard nightingales singing. One day I had embarked on
the little primitive cargo-boat which was then the only means
of transport between Capri and the mainland. The boat was
already very late starting; it bobbed up and down in the swell,
and tugged impatiently at the rope which still held it fast to the
quay. The passengers were sitting crowded together on the
wooden benches, only just above the water's edge, getting
more and more angry. The ship's engine as it chugged away
mixed the smell of oil with that of fish offal, garlic and babes
at the breast. The shimmer of the sea began to make everyone
feel dazed.

Suddenly the shingle crunched; then quick footsteps on the
plank which led from the beach to the boat. Who was this
last passenger, visible to all for one moment, outlined against

* This is the first of the chapters written by Baroness Uexküll.

[67]

the bright shore? His erect, almost stilted carriage was accentuated by the way he held his head thrown back. He had a jutting blonde beard. His clear-cut profile and eyes were hidden by the broad brim of his shabby felt hat. There was something commanding about his presence. His shoulders were narrow; he wore a cape which flapped round him like a dark triangle, under whose folds trotted an enormous Borzoi, so that master and dog made one single strange silhouette. A small white terrier trotted across the plank, adding a finishing touch to the picture.

At that moment the little rusty ship's siren sounded. All the passengers looked at each other and nodded as though to say that everything was all right now. Only one toothless old woman, who was sitting by me, turned to me excitedly and said:

"Yes, yes, that's the Doctor. He's obviously off again to visit some princess or countess: they're always pestering him—they won't have any other doctor but him. I wouldn't have dared ask for him myself, but last winter I was so ill, and he came of his own accord—and, instead of sending me a bill, brought me coffee; no he's not stuck-up, but he's not a money-grubber either—like other doctors."

After greeting the captain, this remarkable stranger had made his way to the ship's bows, where he sat down with his dogs on a coil of rigging. The old sailor, who was his own helmsman, took his pipe out of his mouth in token of respect. He shouted a couple of orders to the young deck hands to haul in the rope, which fell with a clatter on the deck. And then we were out in the open sea.

So that was Axel Munthe, who at that time was beginning to be quite a mythical figure on the island! I myself had not bothered much about the people: sea and rocks; the landscape with its fairy grottoes and endless surprises had cast too great a spell on me. My solitary scourings and exploring trips along the blue-green sea in search of jelly-fish and anemones, and our climbs up to dizzy mountain ridges had been too exciting, and I had felt that time was too short for meeting people.

But one day I was caught, one Thursday reserved for enormous cosmopolitan tea parties in the lovely villa where I was staying. My hostess had just received a visiting-card, and everyone looked surprised and pleased as the name Axel Munthe was passed round. Axel Munthe, the recluse whom everyone knew by sight but very few knew personally, who stubbornly avoided all social intercourse, had suddenly decided to call. " We shan't be bored today, anyway," whispered my hostess to me significantly.

But the gardener's boy, who was still holding the card in his hand, informed our hostess that the doctor did not wish to disturb the company—he only wanted to have one moment's private conversation with her on a somewhat delicate matter.

The private conversation did not take long, and our hostess told us with a laugh that it in no way concerned any of us. The Doctor had heard about Fuchsi, the little golden-brown Pomeranian dog, who was the darling of the house and of a breed very rare at that time. At the sound of his name Fuchsi had sprung up and run over to his mistress, wagging his tail at her expectantly. " Yes, Fuchsi," said our hostess, " you're the attraction, not us; we thought it was us he had come to see. At last you're to be married off suitably; in fact you've been asked to spend a short honeymoon at San Michele, where none of us have ever been." Then she continued, laughing: " The Doctor wouldn't even accept my offer of a cup of tea—he said he was in a hurry. The Crown Princess of Rumania is apparently waiting for him at the garden gate. He said: ' Royalties must find it quite a novel and charming experience to be kept waiting, but one mustn't overdo even that.' "

At that time the lovely Crown Princess of Rumania was

often in Capri; she had artistic talent and used to spend her time painting flowers. Munthe had invited her to do her painting in San Michele—but only when he himself was away! In spite of, or perhaps because of that, she had described him to her sister Melitta as the most fascinating man she had ever met.

A few weeks later we were sitting on the marvellous terrace of the Victoria Hotel in Sorrento. At one of the small tables I saw the man I had first seen on the Capri boat, but this time in a dinner-jacket with a lot of smart-looking people. Supper was over; the terrace was almost empty and in the magic moonlight it seemed to be drifting like a ship in the silvery mist. There was evidently an atmosphere of tension in the little group, for every now and then the stranger would get up and stride impatiently up and down like a caged lion. Perhaps he, too, was lonely in company and somehow felt out of it.

At this time he was working hard in Rome. The only relaxation he allowed himself was sailing. He had to have his little English yacht, the *Lady Victoria*, always anchored ready for him in Anzio harbour, so that he could reach his beloved Gulf in a few hours, either alone with his boatman, Pacciale, or with friends. His friend, Lord Dufferin, the English ambassador, spent a great deal of the summer in Sorrento. Dufferin was also handy with a boat, and had a yacht like Munthe's, so the two friends indulged in many a race together.

Perhaps on that very evening the *Lady Victoria* was waiting on the little mole below to carry its owner over the moonlit gulf to Capri.

After these fleeting impressions years elapsed before I heard any more of Munthe, and even then I did not get to know him personally.

*   *   *

It must have been in 1908. Munthe had come to Berlin

as a member of the Swedish Court. His patient, the Crown Princess Victoria, was now Queen, and the young couple were on a round of visits to various foreign Courts. The 'Unter den Linden' was bestrewn with flags and there was to be a gala dinner at the palace in honour of the Swedish guests.

But the man who had once been the Kaiser's best friend, Prince Philip of Eulenberg, was at the time in Moabit prison, serving a sentence for perjury, ill, shunned and slandered by almost everyone. Eulenberg had enlivened the stiff Swedish Court with his wit and musical talent when he had been German Ambassador in Stockholm, and since then he and the Crown Princess had always been great friends.

Now politics and Court intrigues had banned him from social life, and cut him off from his friends. Even the Kaiser, who till recently had treated him with almost gushing affection, had now abandoned him, which made it particularly embarrassing for the Crown Princess who also had to ignore him. Court etiquette, however, did not worry Munthe. In fact the whole affair must have particularly irritated him; so, armed with a letter from the Queen, he made straight off for the prison, where he found Eulenberg in the sick-ward, the shattering experiences of the last weeks of his trial having made a nervous wreck of him.

Eulenberg reported Munthe's visit at that time in letters to friends, describing in detail the extraordinary man who restored his courage and self-confidence. His gratitude was so great that he actually kept and showed to his closest friends a letter which Munthe wrote to him afterwards.

But meanwhile the palace was being searched for the Doctor, for the Kaiser had demanded a private audience with him. When Munthe finally appeared the terrified courtiers hustled him into the Emperor's study. The Emperor barked out at him: " I've asked twice for you. I'm not used to being kept waiting by my guests. What's kept you so long?"

"Your Majesty—I've been visiting the former German Ambassador in Stockholm."

The only answer to this was a cold stare. After a short silence the Kaiser changed the subject and then abruptly dismissed his guest. But this little scene was soon forgotten, and Kaiser Wilhelm II afterwards always made a point of signalling out his cousin's doctor and talking to him. Perhaps he was intrigued to have at last met someone who dared stand up to him. During his trips to Scandinavia the Kaiser often visited Sweden, and here he and Munthe met again on the occasion of the Queen of Sweden's nomination as Colonel-in-Chief of a German regiment.

The officers were paraded on board the Kaiser's yacht and the Kaiser himself was walking up and down the deck with his cousin. In his usual abrupt way he suddenly called out:

"Where's the Doctor, by the way?"

Highly honoured, the regimental doctor stepped out of the ranks and saluted his Commander-in-Chief.

"No, no!" cried the Emperor. "I mean Munthe."

"That was an awful moment for me," said Munthe later. "I dragged the wilting German quickly to the ship's bar, and stood him whisky after whisky to make him forget what he quite wrongly felt had been a piece of presumption on his part."

The Kaiser's errors of tact which so often gave offence, especially abroad, were not always his own fault. His entourage was largely responsible; by their flattery and kow-towing they created a sort of halo round him, which so dazzled him that in the end he could not see his own way about. One little episode is typical of the behaviour of his suite, who were often more of a hindrance than a help to him. One day he visited San Michele. Let it be said that his knowledge of art was not very great, but before leaving he politely told his host how much he had appreciated all he had seen. One of the members of the Imperial Suite then took Munthe aside and suggested that he present His Majesty, in token of his visit, with the "funny old eagle", a rather sneering reference to Munthe's black cyanite Egyptian "Horus". Now this Horus was Munthe's pride and joy. For years and years the aloof, detached calm expressed by the hard, stylized lines of the falcon god had fascinated him, and driven him to visit countless museums to study specimens of Horus—he had actually had a plaster cast made of a Horus in the Egyptian section of the Berlin Museum. Moreover the mystical function which the Egyptians ascribed to this particular god fascinated him, for the mystery of death obsessed him all his life. He knew all the various forms in which this bird-harbinger of the Gods to the Kingdom of Death were depicted, from the human body with the bird's head to the image of the falcon flying to the underworld and gliding through the lowest vaults of the Pyramids, bringing down food and tidings. Artists have often depicted the bird flying down a small stairway to the lower regions. Munthe had seen and studied all these various conceptions of the falcon, and therefore valued very highly his own black Horus, which, perched on a pedestal, occupied a proud place in the former chapel of San Michele. To him, in fact, the "funny old eagle" was a mythical god, and one can imagine how staggered and at the same time amused he was by the aide-de-camp's proposal.

On his travels as a member of the Queen of Sweden's suite Munthe had many other ludicrous experiences. He described how once in Paris the young King and Queen were received with great pomp. The Republicans had cheered the resplendent young Queen to the echo as she drove through the streets in her state coach. The barber detailed to trim Munthe's hair and beard before the gala dinner, still dazzled by the spectacle, said how wonderful it must be to be a countryman of hers and to be able so often to feast his eyes on her from so close. " Yes, in fact I'm exceptionally lucky," replied Munthe—" I'm her chiropodist."

" The barber was so impressed by the glamour of my Court appointment that he now became almost obsequious in his attentions."

At all Court function sthe Court Physician was supposed to wear special uniform. Munthe hated uniform and cere-monial of any kind and had long discarded his Court dress, though he admitted that the Swedish ' Livmedicus ' dress was remarkably stylish (tradition tells that it originated from the time of the great Linnaeus, and the linnea, the little flower of the Scandinavian forests named after him, was embroidered in gold on it). One day, on his return from England, which he usually visited in spring, Munthe found in his room in Stock-holm Palace this gala uniform complete with accessories, such as cocked hat, sword and buckler, which the Queen had secretly ordered for him. It was the occasion of the King's birthday, and this time the Livmedicus appeared in gala dress.

* * *

Not till many years later, shortly before the First World War, did I get to know Munthe personally. At that time the loss of one of his eyes was a sore burden to him, and he told me he thought he could bear his affliction better far away from the world in his Capri tower of Materita, which he had just bought and fitted out to suit his needs.

Only rarely and for imperative reasons did he seek other people's company. But at that time he had started his " affair " with his Corona typewriter, and one day it had got the better of him. He had sent it straight down to Capri, to a writer friend of his, W. Andrews, asking him to examine it and initiate him more closely into its mechanism.

I myself was at that time on a short visit to Capri. The author Andrews was also an old Capri friend of mine, and I was determined to pay him and his charming wife a visit. On that day, however, I saw to my surprise a notice on his door: " Please first enquire of the maid whether you may come in." In the end, however, I was admitted, and saw that Mr. and Mrs. Andrews were not alone. A stranger in dark glasses was sitting in a corner of the room, his eyes shaded by a broad-brimmed hat. My young hostess said:

" May I introduce Dr. Munthe to you."

Naturally he had no idea who I was, but all awkwardness soon vanished when we began to talk, for we had a great deal in common. Next day or the day after he invited me to San Michele and Materita and showed me round. And because his failing eyesight made him dependent on me, I soon got to know both places pretty well, and gradually learnt something of his life.

A VISIT TO MATERITA

Had there been a visitors' book in Materita people would have been amazed at the strange assortment of guests who were entertained there in the course of the year. The list would have ranged from world-famous figures to people who could not even have signed their names. Apart from royalties, Oscar Wilde, Rilke, Duse and countless other celebrities have had meals at the little refectory table. Artists, writers and occasionally even journalists from all over the world would seek out the hermit in his monastic fortress.

Materita was, indeed, an experience for everyone, and especially for those who came on foot accompanied by the " Signore ". The moment the little iron door which led into the dark oak grove had closed one began to breathe more freely and felt shut off from the noise, hubbub and dust of the outside world. The Doctor would now whistle to his dogs, and immediately Gorm would come bounding up. He would

[75]

welcome one with varying demonstrations of restrained devotion, while we continued our way along the winding paths.

Soon there would be a rustling in the brown foliage, and Lisa would appear. Lisa was a tiny dachsund bitch, and she would wriggle like a golden lizard between the grass and the stones as fast as her little bandy legs would carry her. There was a scent of rosemary everywhere, and of wild Alpine violets, which with their marvellous strength forced their way through the dry, stony autumn soil. They were popularly known as " plate-cleavers ".

There were magnificent views across the grounds of Materita, which were shaded with oaks, pines and olives, and terraced into a series of steep levels. On the lowest level was the cypress-grove, its trees silent and upright; under the cypresses a few marble fragments were dotted about, tombstones of various beloved dogs buried there. Suddenly one would hear the cooing of white turtle-doves, and Munthe would explain that they sang the same love-song the whole year round; fortunately, he would add, his dogs were too well-trained to disturb their romantic dreams. In Materita even the tortoises led a peaceful, idyllic life with their parents and children in a sheltered portico. The baby tortoises, who looked like speckled walnuts, queued up in line for salad leaves. Whenever Munthe was away he would always write to his staff begging them to remember those dumb guests of his, for they too were *pure christiani* (" Christ's creatures ").

A little owl would blink sleepily from its niche in the ivy and underfoot one would hear ring-tailed adders—a harmless breed of snake; there are no poisonous snakes in Capri—searching for their bowls of milk.

A second beautiful wrought-iron gate led to the terrace from which one could see across the still, wide expanse of sea, which gleamed behind the parapet. Old urns adorned the walls, and from elegant clay pitchers sprang a profusion of flowers, which clustered round the pillars.   Then came the sunny fore-court which led to the innermost sanctuary of Materita. Proud, massive and battlemented, the mediaeval tower seemed to look down on us with disdain from its loopholed and embrasured windows, fortress and monastery in one.

Munthe entertained very little.   But that day was Sunday, and every Sunday Maddalena had a standing invitation to lunch at the doctor's house.   She was waiting for him on the terrace.   She was a deformed dwarf with an enormous head and sad dark eyes, and was completely destitute.   She had been an unwanted child—although her family made her do what work she could—and the misery of her life made her permanently welcome at Materita, until she found ultimate rest and peace on Abraham's bosom.   She was sitting in the sun on a low stool, which had been put out specially for her. The dogs knew her well, and were welcoming her in their own rough and ready fashion, pawing her new dress—a wedding garment such as the Prodigal Son received on his return home. Maddalena's small rough hands plucked excitedly and coyly at her head scarf as the *Signore* came up to greet her.   She hardly reached up to his waist.   The two, doctor and dwarf, would have made a typical subject for Velazquez, who, with his peculiar genius, made a special study of dwarf's heads.   He caught exactly the brooding look on the faces of these step-children of nature, when they seem to be pondering on their fate.   *Il Signore* bent down to speak to Maddalena, resting his hand for a moment on her shoulder—a gesture which Velazquez has also immortalized in his painting of the Duke of Spinola bending over his conquered foe, as the latter hands him over the keys of Breda in token of submission.   Here Velazquez has caught the very spirit of humanity—and of chivalry—great verities expressed intimately—and has set down in black and white something which otherwise only the heart could feel, and which the eye could not see.

On entering the tower Munthe found an enormous parcel under his day's mail. It was a present from Germany, where he had made many friends, from the well-known zoologist Hagenbeck who labelled his present "a book of sound-pictures". It was a most sensible and suitable present for Munthe who was nearly blind—a collection of gramophone recordings which Hagenbeck had made during his travels in Africa—of jungle and desert sounds, the rustle of trees in virgin forests, the distant roaring of lions, the shrill cries of rare birds and the chanting of negroes round camp fires exorcising evil spirits. All these sounds and many more combined to form a symphony in which a nature, forceful and incomprehensibly remote, seemed to be talking to itself in primaeval utterance. To the lonely man in the old tower, leaning back with closed eyes in his Savanarola chair and listening absorbed to the mingled sounds, the wordless message of the records seemed more significant than human speech.

Everything in the room seemed to be listening to this weird encroachment of the virgin forest into the monastic silence of Materita—all those images which here surrounded Munthe and with which he had peopled his world. The austere Spanish Madonna seemed to smile faintly, as though at a vision of Paradise before the fall of man. Clearly since the days of the monks' incantations no sound but whispered conversations or the soft hum of a human voice and the gentle notes of a piano had disturbed the air. The small, gracefully carved Madonna on the little table seemed to clasp the child Jesus closer to her breast lest He be startled from his blissful sleep. The ever-burning lamp reflected the small silver triptych which represented St. Michael with drawn sword, prepared, it seemed, at any moment to challenge the primitive, chaotic powers which these jumbled human and animal noises seemed to symbolize. This little picture was Munthe's favourite, and he would often take it down and tell me its history. He had acquired it at the

Axel Munthe at Francesco's wedding, Capri

Maria Porta–Lettere at the age of 80

Court of the late Czar. The Czarina had brought it down from her apartments to show him, believing it to be an old Russian primitive. But with his one good eye, which often saw things which escaped people with normal sight, the Doctor took one look at it and declared that it was of Dutch origin. He was adamant about this. The following day the Czar had had old records searched and discovered that the picture was originally the property of Peter the Great, and that he had either acquired or bought it during his stay in Holland. Before he left the Czarina had given Munthe the little silver painted shrine as a souvenir.

The large classic bronzes, which stood on five marble pillars in the shadows of the vaulted room, gazed enigmatically at the scene they knew so well, surprised at this apparent sudden intrusion of the jungle into their midst. Then the primaeval forest noises suddenly ceased. The chime of an old grandfather clock recalled us to reality. The doctor seemed to be waking from a trance, and as though still under a spell, declared that real figures had appeared to him while the jungle sounds were crowding in on him. When the clock finished chiming the silence seemed deeper than before, as though the room needed a little time to recover its normal voice. Only the colours of the old carpets which time had mellowed now shone in the lamplight. Dusk had fallen, and even the Doctor's footsteps were inaudible as he walked over to the piano.

The Bechstein was nearly always open, and hardly a day passed but its owner played on it. At this time he was threatened with total blindness and was busy learning his favourite songs by ear, so that if need be he could play without music. Music scores, dog-eared and torn, were piled high beside the piano—Bach, Mozart, Wagner, Brahms, Hugo Wolff and, above all, his beloved Schubert.

But this time he did not need any music score. He struck a couple of chords and then began to sing one of his favourite

Schubert songs, at first humming it softly and then breaking
out into his full, clear baritone:

" Du holde Kunst, in wieviel grauen Stunden . . ."

Perhaps no one really knew Munthe until they had seen and
heard him at the piano. His renderings were as moving as the
melodies themselves. To an exceptional degree his own
sensibility fused with that of the composer, and this seemed to
give the compositions new life. He very rarely sang in
company. It was a compliment to be allowed to listen to
him, for he really played and sang for his own enjoyment
alone. He would allow only his most musical friends to
accompany him. One of these was his old friend Dr. Dressler
of Karlsruhe. I recollect in particular one Mozart evening.
Dressler, who was himself very musical, was always pleased
when the Doctor suggested an evening of music *à deux* and the
two had agreed on a composer whom they both loved. The
Doctor, acting as conductor, would place one hand on Dressler's
shoulder and dictate to him his prestos, adagios and pianissimos.
Dressler would often say how the pressure of Munthe's long
fingers on his shoulder inspired him, and express delight at his
singing of *Don Giovanni*.

Munthe and the Queen would also have musical evenings
together, for the Queen had studied under Mottl and had
talent. Dressler was physician-in-ordinary to the Court of
Baden. This was the link between her and the little
Geheimrat as she nicknamed him, and on one of her trips
to Italy she took him with her to Anacapri and Materita. He
was actually the Queen's guest in Casa Caprile, but while he
was there Munthe asked him to spend a few days at Materita,
where the two could sing and play together to their hearts'
content. The whole world of Materita must have seemed a
fairy tale to Dr. Dressler, artist that he was.

Munthe loved showing his treasures to his friends, and was
delighted when they were really appreciative. He could then

truthfully say: "You've really seen and understood that."
And how could anyone not see and appreciate what Munthe
himself showed? Old Venetian glass, in which the red Capri
wine was served, wrought-iron chandeliers, whose shadows
were reflected in fantastic patterns on the walls, and hand-
wrought copper pots and pans in the scullery of the old
monastery kitchen—a dazzling assortment indeed! Visitors
were bewildered when they first entered the two large rooms
in which their host had arranged what seemed to him most
interesting, for they contained ancient and modern master-
pieces collected from all over the world. And yet none of
these treasures seemed out of place. Commenting on this
motley display, one visitor to Materita, a man of some taste,
remarked that at first he was puzzled how such an extraordinary
assortment of objects should harmonize so well. Then, as
the party was breaking up, Munthe had suddenly pointed to a
skull dating from the time of the first Roman Emperor and
said: "Those eyes saw Tiberius." His guest explained later
that he then realized that the mysterious connecting link was
a fairy tale which Munthe in his mind's eye saw, through time
and space, and with which his own life was in some way
bound up. Propped against the wall, under one of the many
Madonnas, was the old ice-pick which had saved his life when
he had fallen into a crevasse during an ascent of Mont Blanc.
Nearby stood Aknaton, guarded by a black Anubis and,
opposite, another early Madonna, with such a sweet, natural
smile that one knew that the artist had been trying to
reproduce the features of some human being whom he had
loved. By one of the pillars which supported the high arch
was a prie-Dieu adorned with a figure of Saint Anne. The
figure rose above the image of the Virgin Mary as a child,
who, wrapped in the folds of her mother's white marble
cloak, was portrayed gazing piously up at her and listening
intently to her reading aloud from a large open book. At the

far end of the vaulted room stood a large, round table with books spread out on it and a couple of arm-chairs, and a little faun on a pedestal, still dreaming of the golden age in which the great Pan flourished. It was only a torso, but seemed as lively as in the days when it pirouetted in exuberant dance with its face turned towards its tail.

When Munthe started to furnish this room the old oil-mill was still there, with the enormous stone basin in which the Cistercian monks used to press the olives. Now the old boarded floor was bestrewn with brightly coloured carpets and rugs, and the plain, white-washed walls and arches cast a gentle light over this fairy world. A small staircase flanked by two red marble lions led into the world of reality.

A terrace led to the small guest-house where the *Geheim-rätchen* spent a few pleasant weeks alone with his host. This terrace was put entirely at his disposal; his morning coffee would be brought to him there, after which he was left alone, to read or dream to his heart's content.

Dressler, who was rather over-trustful, had left his luggage in Naples, where he lost all trace of it for several days. The Doctor could not help teasing him about this. One morning early he was strolling on the terrace and noticed his guest's diary lying open on the table. He did not glance at the previous entries, but took advantage of Dressler's absence to continue them. On his return the little *Geheimrat* stared at the book in amazement. It was closed, but a fresh rose had been placed as a book-marker between the pages, and, on opening the book, he saw his host's unmistakable handwriting. In his somewhat clumsy German Munthe had written:

" Max Dressler. . . . Notes from my diary. October in Anacapri. . . .

The ship glided slowly out of Santa Lucia harbour. Gulf of Naples in dazzling sunshine. Cloudless sky, calm blue sea. There, up above, is old Vesuvius smoking his morning pipe, and down below at his feet lie the white villages of Herculaneum and Pompeii, sleeping their thousand-year sleep. To the east, like a sentry gleaming silver over Sorrento's orange groves, one can see the snow-covered Monte St. Angelo, while far in the distance, veiled in a pink haze, the Siren island is awakening.

No luggage to worry about. . . .

Monday

This old tower is handsome, but looks grim, forbidding and impervious, in fact typically mediaeval. And the man who lives here in gloomy solitude is grim and forbidding too. When I first met him in Karlsruhe he seemed a very modest old man, a bit naive but honest and harmless enough. My illusions have been shattered. I'm an unarmed prisoner in this old tower, bound and helpless, in the hands of a fourteenth-century tyrant. He says it's the result of insomnia, but I realize more and more that it's his nature to order people about and I'm beginning to sympathize deeply with his former patients. He told me himself that the people here call him Tiberius, and I can quite understand it.

I've heard dark tales of strangers, Germans among them, coming to pay him friendly visits and disappearing without trace; when he was younger I gather he hurled a lot of them over the cliffs into the sea.

The food's good here, but very plain, and there might be a bit more of it. Unfortunately one virtually mayn't utter a word at meals; he makes one gobble down everything in a moment, and one hardly knows what one's eating. Yesterday at dinner I was holding forth about various philosophies, from Pythagoras to Kant, when my host pointed to the plateful of food in front of me and merely said: ' Go on, eat.'

I shut up at once and gobbled down my macaroni. Meanwhile my host explained that eating is a physiological need, not a pleasure, and that a man's life is too short to spend half-an-hour a day carefully spreading salt on bread and butter as though it were prussic acid.

Luckily I'm often invited to meals with the Queen, where I can eat away to my heart's content, and like a snake stuff enough into my belly to last twenty-four hours.

One gets wine here ' quantum satis ', but there again—one hasn't time to enjoy it. Last night I was holding my old Venetian wine-glass in my hand and becoming more and more eloquent in my attempts to clarify interpretations of that enigmatic passage in the second part of Faust, when my host said suddenly: ' You've got five minutes to finish that glass of wine:' and five minutes later we left the dinner-table.

After dinner I read Faust aloud to him and his poor secretary (she looks rather thin, which doesn't surprise me), but I'm afraid he doesn't appreciate its immortal beauty and depth. Last night I was declaiming the Angel Chorus with great feeling, and suddenly noticed him sitting fast asleep in his chair like a child.

He's intolerably restless, and has a habit of striding up and down without speaking—indeed he often doesn't even answer when I speak to him. He says one should always walk quickly, as Death pursues one the whole day, step by step, and, when one can no longer walk, seizes one by the back of the neck and hurls one on the ground.

Wednesday

Yesterday my host chivvied me about over his other lovely house, San Michele, but unfortunately allowed me no time to study, take notes, discuss, classify or even admire the wonderful view and all the antiques.

I wanted very much to go to Pompeii, and Tiberius agreed

to this, but said I couldn't do the journey alone. He said that since my carelessness about my luggage on the way here from Naples he had lost all confidence in me. He said that since the day, two thousand years ago, when Tiberius landed on the island, no human being had ever shown such incapacity in dealing with his luggage, and that San Gennaro's only real miracle was getting me on to the island at all.

Thursday

Early this morning, just as I had got out of bed and was walking calmly up and down my private terrace, clad in my host's old red dressing-gown, lost in thought, watching the rays of the morning sun rise from the sea and climb slowly over the rocks, the secretary suddenly appeared with a stern ultimatum from her master: I was to put on my trousers at once or I should get rheumatic fever.

Meine Ruhe ist hin—meine Ruhe ist hin.
Friday . . ."

Dressler enjoyed being teased by the Doctor, and was always pleased when he was in a good mood. He could well appreciate the other's humour, though it was very different from his own. He had, in fact, christened himself Sancho Panza and his host not ineptly Don Quixote.

FRIENDS IN CAPRI

On the island which Munthe made his home there are still some old folk who remember him as he was in their youth; their faces always light up when they begin to talk of him.

There is, for instance, his fisherman friend Francesco, who, with Pacciale, immortalized in the book, *San Michele*, accompanied the Signore on many of his adventurous cruises. The photograph of Francesco's wedding still adorns his little white-washed room, and the Doctor and a young painter are pictured standing beside the black-eyed bride. The photograph is unusual, for Munthe always had a horror of the camera; although at that time he himself possessed a gigantic Knox-kamera and took very good photographs, he always hated being in the picture himself.

The photograph of Francesco's wedding is rather amateurish, but one can tell pretty well from it what Munthe must have looked like then. He is sporting a beret, and with his lean face and blond beard he looks a typical Parisian artist of the period. Francesco tells a good story about the Doctor as he was then. One day he had a specially good catch, and the shallow creel which he had brought into the kitchen seemed to reflect every colour of the rainbow. There were Occhiate with large dark eyes, steel-coloured Angulie like thin-bladed daggers and evil-looking Scorfani like red Chinese armorial dragons with fins spread out. Munthe went into the kitchen to admire the catch, while Assunta, Francesco's wife, was preparing the fish soup for him and his friend Coleman, the painter. The " still life " on the marble slab on the kitchen table enchanted both artists, and Munthe could not help examining closely each fish in turn. In so doing he grazed his finger on one of the razor-sharp fins. No one took it very seriously at first—it looked like a mere pin-prick. But soon Munthe realized that, for all its beauty, the Scorfano is as evil as it looks, and went off to the chemist to have the finger disinfected.

He then returned to Francesco's cottage with his finger bandaged. But his host looked dubious. " No, Signore," he said, " you know nothing about these things. I'm a fisher-man and I know that chemist's concoctions are no antidote to these red devils' poison. You'd better let me deal with it— I know what to do."

But the Doctor thought he knew best. His finger got worse

and worse and began to hurt so much that he had to bite his lips and start stamping about. On the next day the finger looked so angry that the Signore asked Francesco what his " old fisherman's remedy " consisted of. " Just you leave it to me—you'll see," was the answer. The Doctor followed Francesco into his little room, where the fisherman—as he himself puts it, " did the necessary ". That's all he will say; and if people are curious and want to know more he only adds: " Good words—God's words." Francesco, now eighty years old, always ends this story with a complacent nod and a smirk at the recollection of having cured the Doctor by his own special fisherman's remedy.

Another of Munthe's many friends was Domenico Arcucci, a prototype of the peasant aristocrat with the instinctive good breeding characteristic of all peasant families who from the twelfth century onwards have planted and tended their vineyards and olive-groves on the same soil. The Arcucci family first appear in the archives of the Certosa of Capri, in which the Counts Arcucci are mentioned as founding a chapel. Domenico was far the best wine and oil producer on the island, so naturally the Doctor, as a young man, sought his advice when he started cultivating the land round Materita. The discussions between the two soon led to friendship, and even today small faded notes—invitations to breakfast at Materita— are among the treasures of Domenico's white cottage.

Munthe formed a similar friendship with Luigi Maldacena of the Torre della Guardia, his nearest neighbour at Materita, whom he always introduced to his friends as the first gentleman of Anacapri. One day, just after the Doctor had been tramping the vineyard with his dogs, Luigi happened to notice that three of his hens were missing. Full of righteous rage, Luigi immediately called on Munthe and threatened to shoot his dogs if such a thing ever recurred. But the Doctor had carefully trained his dogs never to commit " murder " of any

kind, and therefore hotly protested their innocence. Two
days later Luigi happened to catch his own watchdog *flagrante
delicto*, and without a moment's hesitation shot his own dog
dead. Then, somewhat shamefaced, he went and apologized
to the Doctor. Luigi liked to recount how he and the
Doctor made it up at once. To show there was no ill feeling
the Doctor had given him a walking-stick made of scented
cherry wood, similar to one which he had himself, and of a
kind unprocurable in Capri. Munthe had a silver band
attached to it, engraved with the date of the hens' death.
Luigi always used the stick on his walks until he became too
decrepit to walk at all. And by that time the pebbly roads
had snapped the end right off and it was a mere stump.

But from now on the two men trusted each other completely. To quote an instance of this: every Christmas an
enquiry was held and a printed list made of the villagers most
in need of Poor Relief. Just before Christmas day Munthe
presented this parish list to Luigi whom he considered the final
arbiter. The latter would put on his spectacles, and only his
conscientious additions and erasures would satisfy the Doctor,
after which the money would be doled out.

Almost every day about midday Munthe used to take long
walks with his dogs. He often went down to the lighthouse,
and in summer used to go swimming in the sea with his dogs.
The old lighthouse-keeper would nearly always come out to
talk to him. Apart from these meetings with Munthe he led
a hermit's life, entirely cut off from the world up above, and
was always thrilled to hear the latest news and read the newspaper which the Doctor never failed to bring him in his pocket.

On the days when Munthe's walks took him up past the
Guardia Tower he often called at the little white house in
Luigi's vineyard. He always arrived when Luigi was busy
cooking lunch for himself and his eleven children. The
Doctor would suddenly be spied standing in the shadow of

the pergola where the family were gathered round the enormous bowl containing the broth. It smelt so good, the Doctor would say, that he had been tempted in entirely by the smell, and would love to taste it. An extra plate and glass were produced immediately—Luigi was renowned for his wine— and when the meal was over Marianina would rise and in her charming voice sing a few folk-songs in honour of their guest.

Munthe's blind eye had forced him to retire to Materita with its shady groves. His medical practice was now almost entirely confined to the peasants and fisher-folk of the island. It was quite an experience to accompany him on his rounds through the village. In one of the alleys lived a half-insane old man, who used to vent his maniac rages on his wretched wife. The Doctor had known him in his happier days and now used to visit him fairly regularly. If one stood in the doorway one could hear the magic incantation with which the Doctor tried to exorcise the evil spirit which possessed the man. " You mustn't beat your wife—you mustn't beat your wife," he would repeat over and over again in the same monotone. This incantation would work wonders for a while, and the wife would be left in peace; but soon another messenger would arrive with another urgent summons for the Doctor.

Sundays in Materita were always special occasions. The copper pots and pans in the old kitchen would be furbished up and Rosina would adorn the portrait of St. Antony with fresh flowers. As the small clock tower chimed the hour of noon the Doctor would arrive back punctually from his morning walk. This hour was always reserved for visitors from the village. Often Philomena would be waiting for him, with a touching smile of childlike gratitude on her face. She was still handsome, and, like a Caryatid, always carried a basket on her head filled with nuts, figs and grapes, presents for her host.

Philomena, who can only speak in Capri patois, cannot really describe her attack of paralysis after the birth of her last child, and how no one could cure her. She had lain on her back, motionless and apathetic, for over six years, until at last one day her husband had begged the Doctor to come and examine her. And so it came about that he visited her daily. Soon she began to stop taking her medicines, after which he would merely stroke her forehead and suggest to her how lovely it would be if she could soon get well and start work again. She would even have another child! And everything happened exactly as he had prophesied.

She looked radiant, and her expression was almost rapturous as she gazed up at him. When he had to go away for the operation on his eye, Philomena felt his loss more than anyone. With tear-filled eyes she said: " If he really leaves us I shall feel the end of the world has come."

Even now Philomena's most treasured possession is a small faded photograph nailed over the marital bed, which itself fills almost the whole room. It is a photograph of the Doctor, as everyone knew him, in his broad-brimmed hat, leaning on his stick and with his sheepdog, Gorm, beside him. Philomena only shows the photograph to intimate friends, and only those who can understand her curious dialect can grasp exactly how this miraculous cure was effected.

One day, when Philomena was already beginning to move about a bit, the Doctor had taken her delicate, emaciated hand in his, looked at her very closely and addressed her very solemnly and seriously. " From now on," he had said, " you'll be able to help others too. Not only will you be able to use your hands for work but also for easing and curing the sufferings of others."

And indeed, apart from her work in the vineyard, Philomena soon found herself fully occupied in other ways. Her hands seemed to possess a wonderful healing power. She could only understand that this was a special gift which the Doctor had bestowed on her and must therefore be something good.

This conviction she now transmitted to those who summoned her to their bedsides and to those who were well enough to come to her and climb the little white steps bestrewn with geraniums and carnations which led up to her cottage.

Philomena from now on accepted and practised her new power as a matter of course. She felt that she could only express true gratitude for the miraculous change that had come into her life by helping others.

Faith in the Signor Dottore's power grew from day to day. He was always being called in to deal with drunkards, to exorcise love-pangs and every imaginable bodily and mental ill. Sometimes the peasants' unbounded faith in him made him uneasy. He could not bear to be pilloried as a quack. And yet had he the right to debunk this simple people's faith in him; was it not an asset which enabled him to bring succour to the hopeless?

He finally decided to ignore the inevitable troubles—among them countless requests for money—which were the price of his almost seer-like position on the island, and always to do his best to solve the many serious complications in other people's lives. But he saw that the reverence with which the islanders treated him had its comic side, and once said jokingly that as the rôle of soothsayer had been forced on him quite against his will he had better retire on specified days to a grotto and there hold court.

So by degrees Munthe became more and more a doctor for the worried or the mentally sick. He very rarely used drugs on them, for he knew only too well what reserves of health sick people possess, and how it can be stimulated to resist the illness. Thus many bottles of medicine disappeared out of many sick-rooms, for the Doctor's orders were that " the Madonna should be allowed to use her powers ".

Many contemporary medical men would have disapproved of his methods. His treatment was certainly in direct opposition to that of one of his colleagues, who had treated a stubborn and somewhat too rich patient so long with medicines and low diet that the relations were about to call in a priest to administer extreme unction. Then Munthe paid a visit to the sick-bed. After examining the patient he calmly and thoughtfully lit a cigarette and said: " I'll go into your hall and finish this cigarette. It won't take me five minutes. In that five minutes you must decide whether you want to live or die. If you want to live you must give up this idiotic treatment; the illness they've diagnosed in your case doesn't exist." The woman took Munthe's advice, and actually outlived the man who saved her.

But Munthe was unusually sceptical not only about drugs but also about his own capacities—indeed about all orthodox medicine. He loved recounting a conversation he had once had with ' Trenta Carlin '. The nickname itself (thirty *carlinen* was the cheapest coin in Old Naples during the Bourbon era) pointed to the fact that the old boy had never got anywhere, especially as he was always drunk. He had asked to see the Doctor to tell him his woes and to beg him for a little money as well. In telling his story he mentioned the fact that only one of his thirteen children was still alive to support him in his old age.

The Doctor's professional interest was aroused.

" But what on earth did all your children die of?" he asked.

" Well, the doctors polished them all off," replied Trenta Carlin calmly, as though doctors were as likely to cause death as any disease.

Winter in Capri was always the hardest season for the poor. For months on end there was no foreign trade, and the heavy rainfall interrupted all building and farm work. Munthe knew all this and knew by name the cottages and families most in need. But now and then there were exceptional cases of hardship, and he was always on the look-out for these.

This constant watchfulness resulted in an incident which became the talk of the village for many years.

In Scandinavia and the north the increasingly brilliant glow of the Advent crown in the candlelight as Sunday follows Sunday is the best reminder of the approach of Christmas. But in the south the heralds most evocative of approaching Christmas are the Zampugnari, or bagpipe players. At this season charabanc loads of curious-looking musicians arrive from the farthest mountain-villages of the Abruzzi to serenade the Infant Christ. They always wear the same old hats which with the years acquire a mossy sheen and soft pastel shades, and which make them look like shepherds in old Christmas cribs. They invade the village in their long, sleeveless cloaks, their legs tightly corded right down to their feet, on which they wear calf-skin shoes corded like sandals.

They travel mostly in pairs, fathers and sons together, their pipes strapped to their backs and bundles of small wooden ladles, which they have carved at home on summer evenings and have now brought to sell. These ladles bring good luck and prosperity to the household. The pipers go from door to door; and you hear them chant their traditional airs from far off: lullabies and roundelays to the Infant Christ, seated among the angels in Heaven's pastures before descending to live among men and tread this desolate earth.

Rainer Maria Rilke spent one Christmas in Capri. When he heard this song he made the singers recite the words, which date from time immemorial, and wrote them down in order to translate them into German.

But the Zampugnari rarely meet poets on their pilgrimages. Most of them only earn enough to pay their rent, while the more fortunate make at best a tiny profit which they take back to their distant mountain villages.

Several years ago one of these old Adventist musicians was taken ill in Anacapri. His relations had all died, so he had had to do the journey alone. One morning the owner of the inn where he was staying found him lying dead in one of the rooms, with his cloak wrapped round him. His landlord and lady were terrified, and furious too, for, having so far earned nothing, he had died without paying. He had not even received the last sacrament. So any form of Mass or Christian burial was out of the question. In life constant poverty and suffering had been his lot, and even in death people seemed to have forgotten that the old piper had been one of those who had serenaded the Infant Christ.

He was still lying there abandoned and the crowd had dispersed shaking their heads and muttering that there was no precedent in a case like this, when Axel Munthe, who had just returned to San Michele, heard the whole story. Hitherto he had always invited the Zampugnari to play at San Michele, and after the performance had offered every one of them a dish of macaroni and a glass of wine. How could he desert an old friend now that he was dead! He must have as gorgeous a funeral as Anacapri could provide; he must have flowers and music, and the whole village must form a procession in his honour! Of course a Mass must be read for him, in which every priest must chant his praises and he, Munthe, must himself be present. There must be no niggardliness; when the music petered out and the priests thought they had performed their office adequately Munthe kept urging the choir on to fresh efforts with his: " *Più forte*—louder!"

This Mass impressed the people of Anacapri not a little; to think that *il signor Dottore* should have ordered it purely to honour the piper from abroad! And they began to wonder; was it the Infant Christ Himself who had prompted the Signore to honour his piper thus? After all, they argued, during Advent the little crib with His carved image had rested awhile in San Michele, as in all the houses of the devout, before being taken to the Church for the festival.

Men and animals

Munthe was an instinctive animal lover. Their ways, their multiformity, their baffling behaviour combined with the fact that they clearly conformed to fixed laws had intrigued him since childhood. He might possibly have had a happier though not so full a life had he devoted himself entirely to them and become either a zoologist or biologist.

Once at a rather lively party someone boldly asked Munthe what had prompted him to become a doctor, when with his many gifts he might equally well have become a successful painter, musician, architect or diplomat—indeed, his cross-questioner insisted, kingship was not beyond his reach. (The people of Capri, in fact, suspected him of being King Gustaf of Sweden's half-brother.) He smiled at the question, thought for a moment, and then muttered half to himself: " I must have had some sort of instinct to rescue people, like a St. Bernard dog."

Apart from the more practical motives for choosing a profession it was clearly what he called his " St. Bernard dog instinct " which decided him. His life could indeed be summarized as a seventy-year-long struggle for men and animals. Pity and a little courage, he used to say, are two infallible guarantees of an adventurous life.

His crusades in defence of those misunderstood, suppressed and ill-used members of God's universe began very early in life and continued to his death. While he was poor his only weapon was his fierce and passionate pen. But these early attacks were by no means the mere scriptural out-pourings of a sentimental youth; he soon followed them up with action—and attacked on all fronts, sometimes with, sometimes without, allies. And now ensued a series of varied and successful campaigns; he might launch out against small-town travelling menageries, or fulminate against the slave-driving of horses, donkeys or dogs, whose sufferings never failed to rouse his ire.

Unfortunately the Latin races are notoriously cruel to animals. There the Church, ever mindful of and concerned for the welfare of its human flock, seems to have forgotten God's other creations—indeed the peasants actually stigmatize them as *Non Christiani*. This particular name for them is so extraordinary that one cannot help trying to guess its origin. Does it mean that animals have no souls and are therefore essentially worthless—or merely that, like the unbelievers in the Crusades, being creatures without faith, they have no claim to human consideration? This cruelty to animals, which is peculiar to Latin races, is all the more puzzling when one thinks what marked kindness Latins, especially Italians, show to one another.

By degrees people began to regard Munthe as a sort of representative of the animal world in the world of men. People wrote from everywhere asking him to see them and help reform some impoverished organization. Once, for example, during an unusually severe winter, a telegram arrived from Sweden asking him to send money at once to help release hundreds of swans, who had been caught by the frost and were ice-bound on a lake. Munthe responded at once to this S O S and sent a money-order by telegram. He heard soon after that his generosity had saved the swans, that an open channel had been found for them, and that they had started on their long flight south, a piece of news which rejoiced his heart for many days. Of the many orders which had been awarded him there was only one he cared about, and which he would take out and gaze at from time to time, a small badge of membership of the Swedish Society for the Protection of Animals, depicting a bird of passage in silhouette on a blue enamel ground.

Munthe's campaign against bird-snaring, especially in

Capri—against nets, traps, children using catapults, and stalking parties setting out at crack of dawn with pointers, setters and rifles—is world-renowned. He had great successes at first, but the campaign finally ended in defeat.

Mussolini was virtually the only man in Italy who backed him. In his preface to the Italian edition of *The Story of San Michele* the author expresses his hope that this crusade for the birds would soon be won: " May my dearest wish be granted—to hear in this miraculous land the chant of the birds join in happy chime with the bells of Assisi." Mussolini was apparently delighted with *The Story of San Michele*, and expressed a wish to meet the author. The meeting took place in a private house in Rome, and not a soul got to hear of it. That day the crowd round the palazzo in question consisted entirely of private detectives. Soon after, however, the Duce decreed that the whole of the island of Capri was to be a bird sanctuary. Munthe was exultant. He had a stone slab erected on his own property, the pine-covered slopes of Mount Barbarossa, bearing the inscription: " The San Michele Sanctuary ", and declared the whole of that beautiful hillside a commonwealth, specially dedicated to his protégés. For his friends, both known and unknown, he wrote a letter which appeared in *The Times* on January 27th 1933:

" Sir,—Is it too much to ask you to be allowed to send a word of thanks through your paper to the great number of English bird-lovers, who have been writing to me by every day's post, ever since Lord Howard's letter to *The Times* about Capri being declared a bird sanctuary? It is not possible for me in my crippled condition to answer personally all these letters, but I feel ashamed to remain silent when so many kind men, women, and children come forth to say that they rejoice with me in the generous and courageous response the Italian Government has given to my humble appeal for clemency on behalf of the migratory birds of Capri. I well knew that England was the country of bird-lovers, but I did not know that I had so many friends among them. Yes, well may they rejoice, for if all goes well this measure means the opening of a new era for bird protection in Italy.

" As I am writing this, a little blackcap is singing under my window at the top of his voice ' La Giovinezza ', the Fascist hymn:

> ' Giovinezza, Giovinezza,
> Primavera di bellezza,
> Il fascismo è la salvezza
> Della nostra libertà.'

Has, then, the rumour of the new decree already been broadcast among you blackcaps and made you cancel your scheduled long-distance flight across the Mediterranean? But really you have no business to be serenading Mussolini this time of year on this island, little blackcapped Fascist! Mussolini is indeed a great magician; he can save the lives of thousands of blackcaps by a single stroke of his pen, and accelerate the rhythm of the heart of a whole nation, but surely he cannot accelerate the rhythm of the sun? Do you not know that winter has come, that the north wind may sweep down upon us any day from snow-capped Apennines? Indeed, you are a courageous little fellow; I am sure you must be a British-born blackcap, the pluckiest of all warblers, eagerly awaiting the first signal of spring to return to the land of your birth. But there is still plenty of time; you had better stay and sing to me till the lizards begin to stir among the ivy leaves and the almond trees in the garden of Materita are in bloom. Do not believe a word the violets and the anemones and the cyclamen say;

they are always mixing up the seasons, always forgetting that winter has come. Do stay with me as long as you can; sing to me of spring, and make me, too, forget that winter has come! I well know you will soon be off, by command of your Maker, to sing, to fight, to woo, to win, to love, to mate, and rear your young. You are going to have a glorious time, little blackcap! I know all about it; I, too, have been young: that is what we were born for, my friend, both you and I. All the rest is of small importance to our Creator. You have also, I know, to fulfil your engagement for the opening of the grand opera season, under the patronage of Almighty God, in every English garden, with subdued nightingale rehearsals at dawn among the rhododendrons under a bedroom window, and gala open-air performances the whole day long, with all the leading stars of the company. Then there are to be popular promenade concerts every evening for the lonely wanderer in the forest among friendly trees, with solos of a belated blackbird singing his ballad late in the night. Then there are to be *matinées* on all the commons, where the greatest lyric poet of all time will sing Nature's glorious morning hymn to the rising sun. Quivering on invisible wings high overhead, his body is so small that a child could clasp it in his hand, and yet his immortal voice is strong enough to fill the whole sky with gladness and every human heart with gratitude.

"Do you know where I saw him last, the sky-born God's Messenger, the sun-worshipper? He was beating his wings against the steel bars of his prison, no bigger than a mouse-trap. His head was drooping, his eyes were half closed in the agony of terror, one of his tiny feet was almost torn off by the string of the snare. Was this, then, to be your reward for all the joy you had given to us? What offence against the laws of God or man had you committed to be condemned to prison for life like a dangerous criminal?

" ' Skylark, six bob. Handsome present for a child. Skylark, six shillings!'

" Yes, you had better go there yourself, to ' Club Row ' bird market any Sunday morning—Sunday of all days! Go there and read with eyes filled with shame and anger this humiliating indictment against the most civilized city in the world, this damning evidence in the hands of a coming enlightened generation that after all we of today were but cruel barbarians.

" ' Skylark, six bob! Handsome present for a child. Skylark, six shillings!'

" You may call it a small matter; you are mistaken, it is a grave matter. The smaller the victim, the greater the crime. What is the use of your preaching the gospel of St. Francis to other nations, less conscious than we of man's responsibility towards the animal world, as long as there is a ' Club Row ' in every big English town? What is the good of us wishing God-speed to your migratory birds on their perilous homeward flight, as long as there is a cage with an imprisoned bird in so many an English nursery?

" When is this ignoble slave traffic of catching and selling wild birds to cease? Have your legislators forgotten your proud record as the freest country in the world? Or why, then, do they not set your captive wild birds free?

Yours faithfully,

AXEL MUNTHE.

Torre di Materita, Anacapri, Bay of Naples."

But the decree was wildly unpopular in Capri itself: the people resented it deeply, and Munthe had to pay dearly for his championship of the birds. Soon after the enforcement of the new law he found both his dogs dead in the park. The villagers had enticed them with tit-bits containing poison thrown to them through the railings. Everyone knew that Munthe would grieve at losing these dogs, for he and they were almost inseparable.

Even strange dogs took to him at once, and he used to say jokingly that all dogs liked to have a sniff or two at him. With his own dogs Munthe always established a firm, clear-cut relationship, with each party's rights and functions clearly laid down. Both parties seemed to have the greatest regard for each other and were equally anxious to read the others' thoughts and wishes, and to fall in with them. When Munthe became almost totally blind he could not help occasionally stumbling over whichever dog happened to be faithfully accompanying him that day. He would apologize at once. " So sorry, Wolf," he would say.

But unlike so many animal lovers, Munthe was no sentimentalist, and always insisted on having his dogs destroyed when they became old and sick, and could no longer enjoy life. He hated parting with them but would have felt guilty if he had allowed them to live on in pain. When his blindness increased and he could no longer do his own " mercy-killing ", he would often ask friends to shoot his own " incurables " for him. But one day after his eye operation, he produced his revolver, went off with Gorm into the park, and returned sadly half-an-hour later.

He was then quite an old man. Gorm was his first German sheepdog, and the last but one of those many dogs who were his constant companions through life. Gorm was typical of his breed, which seems so particularly attuned to the company of human beings. The Queen of Sweden had found and bought Gorm in a Karlsruhe kennels when he was barely out of the puppy stage and given him to Munthe when she reached Rome. But the Doctor was fully occupied attending to his patient, and Rome had no appeal for the young dog; it had no familiar tracks and as yet no scent trails. So he fled at the first opportunity and, when his new master returned from the Queen's sick-room, had vanished into the blue. At Her Majesty's special request the police were urgently alerted and a three days' search was organized without result. Rome was teeming with dog thieves at that time, and any further search seemed futile. Even the Doctor, taking his morning stroll in the Villa Borghese, had become resigned to Gorm's loss. But something almost like a miracle occurred. Munthe happened to be walking past one of the many shrubs in the park when he heard a faint whimper. He turned and walked up to the shrub, where he found Gorm crouched inside, half-starved, hardly able to wag his tail. This last-minute rescue from starvation and death decided Gorm never again to lose track of his master. He was made watch-dog of Materita, a post he stuck to all his life, until his master, in return for years of devoted service, shot him to spare him the pain of an infirm old age.

Munthe's intuitive knowledge of animal psychology is also revealed in his treatment of his dachshund; he realized that one cannot expect of a dachshund the selfless devotion which seems to be inherent in sheepdogs. On their walks together he was always very tolerant with Lisa, his miniature dachshund, allowing her to run about as she liked; for, as he expressed it, she seemed to have so many affairs of her own to settle and always to have some fresh schemes in her head. Her schemes were usually concerned with catching mice, and yet whenever she chose to appear above ground, her ears a-flutter, Munthe always had something nice to say to her. In the end he found her a husband, a miniature dachshund like herself, of equally distinguished stock, who travelled, with a lackey as escort, all the way from the Royal Palace in Rome to Materita, where they were to be married. On Christmas Eve of all days Lisa produced five replicas of herself, each the size and colour of a breakfast-roll.

In Anacapri the peasants still tell the story of the dog with rabies; this animal used to attack the vineyard workers during the day, causing them great inconvenience and loss of working hours in their attempts to shoot it. At night it would take refuge in the cellar of a ruined house, where no one dared follow it. Panic spread through the village, and finally a small deputation went to Materita to ask the Signore to help them deal with the situation. The Doctor no sooner heard the story than he took out his revolver and loaded it. It was getting dark, but luckily two of the men had brought lanterns to light the way, and the three of them climbed the hillside to the sinister ruin, from which issued periodic, long-drawn-out howls. The flickering lantern-light could not penetrate the cellar's dark depths, but the Doctor, nothing daunted, entered alone, carefully feeling his way along the walls. Hardly had his eyes got used to the darkness when the dog sprang at him from a corner, foaming at the mouth. The next moment it collapsed mortally wounded.

Munthe was always delighted to meet strangers from the animal world, but, as he himself confessed, did not always enjoy meeting new people. Once in Rome, for instance, he went so far as to hire a tame performing bear from a Gipsy, merely to give the bear a pleasant day's outing, and, as he himself confessed, to spend a few hours in such unusual and delightful company. When his friends saw him and the bear driving along in an open carriage seated side by side and entering the inn together like two old friends, they were naturally amazed. The two sat face to face at a reserved table in a corner of the room, the Doctor and his guest differing only in their appetites. All travelling showmen had lately suffered from a pretty bad slump in trade, and the bear was, of course, delighted for once to be able to eat his fill.

One day Munthe even insisted on taking a little sucking-pig by the leg, observing it closely and then saying laughingly, " I had no idea pigs were so nice!"

Munthe has himself described his interest in monkeys. They fascinated him all his life, from little hurdy-gurdy monkeys and the well-known consumptive gorilla he has immortalized in *San Michele* to Billy, that enterprising rascal who drank down whole bottles of wine, tried his hand at painting and finally was suspected of arson in a church. When Patti landed in Capri Munthe acquired a new simian acquaintance.

Patti was copper-coloured and came from Siam. His serious little monkey-face was surrounded by a bristling mane. Generations of careful breeding had accentuated these traits, and this rare breed was only to be found at the Siamese Court. The purity of the strain was jealously guarded, and no *mésalliance* was allowed. The King of Siam actually gave one of his guests, an Englishman, a scion of this breed of ' blue-blooded ' gibbons as a special favour, because the Englishman had promised the baby ape a happy future and an honoured place in his famous private zoo in Monmouth Park. Lord Tredegar and the ape managed the return journey quite well until they reached Capri, but here the little creature obviously began to lose heart. It turned up its nose at the food and clung trembling to its master's neck. Tredegar was very worried, and in his search for medical advice suddenly thought of Axel Munthe, the celebrated animal lover, who luckily happened to live on the island.

A telephone had just been installed at Materita and suddenly an English voice was heard down the wire, that of Lord Tredegar, asking to come and call on the Doctor. Would the Doctor allow him and his protégé, a monkey, to pay him a visit? At that time Munthe had given up his practice and saw very few people, so it was on the cards that the monkey would be received and His Lordship shown the door. However both were allowed in, and the Doctor actually had a solution ready. He knew one of the very few animal-lovers in Capri, who only a short time before had organized with Lady Algernon Gordon-Lennox the first horse-show on the island, in which prizes were given to all cab-drivers who could show that their horses were reasonably well cared-for. Signora Trama had no children, but all the more love and understanding for animals—and, strangely enough, she also had a monkey. So the two men made their way to her with their patient, and asked if she would take him in as a paying guest, as he was not fit to travel and as his master had already booked a passage to England.

So Patti took up residence in the little white house where, restored to health by careful nursing, he won his foster-mother's heart. Soon everyone was amazed to see a Moses basket with a pale-blue lining being carried into the house and placed next to the large double-bed. Patti was clean and so well-brought-up that he was soon given bedclothes with his name embroidered on them. Punctually every evening he put himself to bed, pulled the sheets over him and slept till morning. It was his foster-mother's habit to ring every morning at a stated hour for the maid to bring her her first cup of black coffee, to which she was fatally addicted. Patti, however, had other ideas, and soon got hold of the bell himself; he would clutch it with both hands and press the knob with his lips. This inspired technique was his own invention. If the maid didn't come at once he pressed the bell again, but never monkeyed about with it wantonly. He thoroughly enjoyed the morning ablutions which followed and helped enthusiastically by taking his little wash-basin to the bucket to empty it. Then his coat was brushed with Bay Rum, so that he was free of vermin. Munthe would not at first believe the reports of such simian refinement, but later visited the house every day and got first-hand evidence. Regular bulletins about Patti's progress and health were sent to England, and Lord Tredegar was so encouraged by these that he decided to return himself to Capri to bring Patti home. But gradually Patti reached the 'wild oat' age! He would sit on the balcony in the sun and watch his young human contemporaries below waving up at him and laughing. In contrast his nursery, with its perch, swing and sand-pen, seemed like a prison, and one day he suddenly slid down the trellis. The young street urchins welcomed him with shouts of joy, and, holding his blue nightshirt up in his hand like a skirt, he started pirouetting about in front of them.

After this escapade Patti was declared of age, and Lord Tredegar decided to come to Capri to stay with him a few days before taking him back to England; this seemed the best way to make friends with him and to wean him from petticoats and apronstrings. The Englishman was delighted to see his gibbon again, this time so well and in such good spirits, and ordered a suite in the hotel to accommodate them both. After his last escapade Signora Trama had bought Patti a smart waist-band with a long lead attached, which Tredegar thought unnecessary and likely to irritate him. But the opportunity now offered for breaking away proved too tempting for Patti and Signora Trama's good upbringing failed in spite of it. Patti was now fully grown and up to so many tricks that the hotel management politely requested Lord Tredegar to remove his ape. Tredegar, in despair, at once appealed to Munthe to protest against such a ridiculous prejudice on the part of the hotel.

Shortly afterwards Munthe was standing angrily at the Hall Porter's desk, but what the porter told him made even him doubtful. Patti, it transpired, had climbed out of the window in the night, crossed the open verandah, got into another room, settled himself on the chest of a woman suffering from heart trouble, who was in bed asleep, and begun tousling her hair with his long, thin fingers. The woman woke up, saw the gruesome creature reflected in the moonlight and let out an unearthly shriek. The whole hotel had been disturbed, declared the Porter; a doctor had had to be summoned in the night and it would apparently take weeks for the lady to recover from her nocturnal visitation. After this Tredegar decided after all not to take his protégé to England. Signora Trama was overjoyed, and took over Patti for good and all, as one of her family.

Axel Munthe was never very talkative, and was often lost in thought. But in certain moods he would open his heart and describe strange and unaccountable events in his life. I will relate one of these as nearly as possible in his own words:

" I was working very hard at the time and used only to visit Capri in my yacht for a few weeks every summer. San Michele was already habitable, and I had also bought the mountain with the old pirate Barbarossa's ruined fortress. High up on Barbarossa's mountain there was also a St. Michael's chapel, with a small hermitage inhabited many centuries ago by a monk. Now I had a camp-bed in what used to be his cell, and in the evenings after sunset I would often walk up there to sleep, when the nights were too sultry in San Michele. All I would take with me was a bottle of Capri wine, and some bread and cheese. The world was far off, shrouded in a blue haze, and I was alone with my thoughts. Often an eagle-owl's hoot sounded—long-drawn-out and eerie. There it was, that wonderful bird, audible only to the night and the mountain, and I felt somehow that I was intruding in its domain. I have always loved owls—in Rome I had a pet owlet. But by degrees the eagle-owl seemed to tolerate my presence; I heard its hoot nearer and nearer and from time to time the muffled beat of its wings would sweep low over the balcony where I was sitting under the stars.

"On one particular evening I climbed up to my hermitage; the weather was unsettled, and my experience as a seaman warned me that the dead silence of that summer night was somehow ominous. That night the owl did not hoot. I lay down in my cell and slept for perhaps two hours; then suddenly I heard the owl's hoot very loud and right up against my open window. I looked out; everything was as peaceful as usual; only the great eagle-owl swooped down again once or twice softly over my cell. The owl had stopped hooting now, and yet I felt someone or something—I don't know what—warning me to get up and leave the place. I dressed and—as though under compulsion and half surprised at myself for doing so—climbed down the mountain path through the dark, velvety summer night between shrubs of myrtle and broom, in which I heard crickets chirping. When I got back to the house everyone was fast asleep; no one heard me coming in, and I felt my way in the dark up to my bedroom.

"On waking next morning I noticed that the wistaria round my window was rain-soaked. I climbed up the mountain again, this time with my old boatman, Pacciale, walking ahead, to fetch some things I had left in my cell the night before. We reached the mountain top, and I was about to follow the road which led to the chapel when Pacciale came stumbling towards me. His face was chalky white, and his knees were trembling. 'What on earth's the matter?' I asked him. He could only stutter: 'Vedete Signore; just go and look.' When I reached the top I saw what had happened: there had been a thunderstorm in the night; a thunderbolt had struck the chapel, covered my bed with rubble and hurled an enormous block of stone at the head of it—a deadly, well-aimed blow!

"Neither Pacciale nor I said a word. Pacciale crossed

himself. I could read his thoughts: Saint Michael, who had so often guided us home from our dare-devil yachting trips, had again protected me. But I remembered at once—and have never forgotten—the mysterious warning voice which, not for the first time in my life, had saved me."

On still nights the eagle-owl's sombre hoot can still be heard across the valley from Monte Solaro's slopes. From time immemorial this lovely bird has rightly been regarded as the symbol of wisdom. What do we know of its secret understanding with the hidden forces of Nature?

Red Cross and Iron Cross

MEN OF GENIUS AND IMAGINATION, WHO ALSO POSSESS strong feelings, tend to be prejudiced. They do not take experiences and impressions at face value, pigeon-hole and draw straight-forward conclusions from them, but allow their imaginations to distort them and give them some special, personal significance. They regard the world as an arena, and are not content with the rôle of interested but detached spectators, watching from the gallery. A man of feeling and action like Axel Munthe could not help reacting strongly and vividly to events. And the Don Quixote strain in him would then be spontaneously aroused, and he would take up the cudgels instantly.

Even his attitude to politics was often determined by spontaneous feeling rather than by cool reasoning. One subject which he could not judge objectively was German politics, and he would make hypothetical formulations of a ' German character '. His sweeping and often unjust views on this subject may have sprung from a lack of fundamental knowledge of Germany's problems. But his idealism and glory in combat never allowed him to ride past a ' windmill '. And the strength of his feelings about Germany may have been due to events which had influenced him in his youth.

When he was a student in Paris, France was still under the spell of the 1870 war. That war, though waged more humanely than present-day wars, which are more like mechanized earthquakes, was still bitterly resented everywhere in France; moreover the Republic still had the charm of novelty, and monarchy and imperialism, which were once more coming into force beyond the Rhine, were regarded as retro-gressive movements towards feudal barbarianism. So in French student and Bohemian circles, where Munthe felt himself most at home, opinion of Germany was low.

Italy was his second great experience. Her sunshine, beauty and art appeared to his Norseman's eye like a *Fata Morgana*. A country in which there were still highway-men with whom one could hob-nob as in fairy-tales, and where the people, however poor, were content, friendly and approachable, was bound to appeal both to his adventurous streak and to his love of homely, uncomplicated human beings. At first he devoted his time mostly to the poor, but his practice in Rome very soon led to his being consulted by diplomats and royalties.

It was in Rome that he began to mix and make friends with the members of the English colony, which at that time numbered some notable figures. He himself, in his *Story of San Michele*, describes practically nothing except his medical practice and the various patients who consulted him. But anyone who knew him in Rome at that time still remembers his enchanting conversation and quick wit. He was one of the most popular members both of Roman and foreign society.

He later paid several visits to England in the great days of her prosperity, where he met many eminent Englishmen. The charm and hospitality of the English country houses, the long-standing tradition of gentleman-like upbringing, which made Englishmen models of behaviour to the rest of the world, his friendships with distinguished diplomats and writers—all combined to make him, as a foreigner, feel that here at last was a country which maintained the highest standards, which other nations should follow. He later married an Englishwoman, and his sons were educated in England as Englishmen.

S.A.M. [III]

This love of England explains the fact that, though Sweden was neutral in the First World War, Axel Munthe sided passionately with the Entente, and although nearly sixty and half-blind, at once offered his services to the British Red Cross.

His experiences in French and Belgian field-hospitals inspired him to write that book of war-memoirs which was reviled at the time in Germany, but which appeared in England under the title of *Red Cross and Iron Cross*. Men's hate instincts are the ugly reverse side of their love impulses, and it was clearly love of England alone which inspired Munthe to write this book, and inevitable that he should write from a biased standpoint, that of Germany's enemies at the time.

How far wrong or biased judgments lower a man's value in our eyes is a question which each must decide for himself. We need only touch on it here to show how easily even people of real merit and integrity are swept away by national passions, and lose their faculty for cool assessment. Munthe's war book was widely read in England, but was not heard of in Germany for some time. Soon after its appearance the author had qualms about fresh editions being published. In any case he refused categorically to allow it to be translated into French and other languages. Perhaps his conversation with some English officers at the St. James's Club in London, which he himself reports, had caused him some misgivings. This conversation illustrates well the English sense of ' fair play '. The young officers had just come back from the front, where one of them had lost an arm. Munthe's war book, vilifying the enemy, seemed to them ' un-English '. Front-line soldiers usually have no sympathy for hating people in the mass, regarding it as evidence of a tame and stay-at-home spirit.

In time the Germans naturally got to hear of the book, though it was only discussed among a small circle. The

German propaganda machine had by that time also been set in motion and there were lively discussions about it in the newspapers, for Axel Munthe had meanwhile become known and admired in Germany as the author of *The Story of San Michele*. Furious protests appeared in the German press, and it looked as though *The Story of San Michele* would be submerged in the tide of indignation against the war book.

Some of the attacks on the author were unfortunately in the worst of taste, the most insulting being a leading article in the *Völkischer Beobachter*, which quoted extracts from the book and was headed " The *Lump* of San Michele ".

Such attacks naturally tickled Munthe's sense of humour. He pressed his German friends for the most exact translation of the word *Lump*, and, finding that there was no adequate rendering of the word, he signed all his letters to Germany shortly and laconically: " The Lump " (or " the scallywag "). He vaguely remembered having read the word years before in Goethe, in the context: *Nur die Lumpe sind bescheiden* (" only scallywags have no stirrings of pride ").

Before *The Story of San Michele* was published in Germany Munthe had already started his scheme for founding an institute for German war-blinded soldiers. But, as it turned out, this purely disinterested and charitable work exasperated the German jingoists still more. A group of German doctors immediately started a rival collection with the sole object of casting Axel Munthe's charity " back in his teeth ". A letter which Munthe received from Germany proved that the doctors' zeal was not entirely altruistic, and that there were many unprejudiced men among them who saw through and disapproved of their policy. The letter ran as follows:

" MY DEAR COLLEAGUE,

" You are bound to have heard by now that there has lately been a press campaign in Germany against your

' Story of San Michele ', instigated by doctors who hav
read your war book ' Red Cross and Iron Cross '. Thi
is all the more surprising because the medical journa
Das Hörrohr [' The Stethoscope '] was full of praise fo
your San Michele book.

"I myself am a book lover . . . and, like yourself, a
doctor. So I hope you will excuse this short letter, whicl
may be of use to you. . . .

"Your book ' Red Cross and Iron Cross' was writter
under the influence of war psychology, which I can under
stand. Many similar books have appeared in Germany
whose authors, I feel sure, regret having written as the
did then, under the influence of war-fever, and would writ
in quite a different spirit today. *Intra muros peccatur e
extra.*

"None of this, however, explains why the Germar
medical profession started this press campaign against you
And I think I should enlighten you about this, and try t
convince you that this outburst on the doctors' part is
mere ' storm in a tea-cup '.

"For several years now German doctors have beer
trying to establish close contact with the Government; ir
fact they seize every opportunity to prove their submissive
ness to the régime. Moreover the two leading medica
associations, the *Hartmannbund* in Leipzig and the *Aerzte
vereinsbund* in Potsdam, rival each other in servility. Toda
nationalism is all the rage in Germany. You must hav
heard echoes of the war-mongering speeches of Hitler anc
others across the Alps.

"I would like to state here *en passant* that a large per
centage of German doctors disapprove of this tendenc
on the part of the profession, for they foresee that not onl
individual practitioners but the profession as a whole wil
lose their independence. . . .

[114]

" Astonishing on the face of it that the German medical profession should have started a subscription list merely in order to return you your ten thousand mark endowment for the war-blinded! It must appear petty indeed to anyone who does not know the political issue behind it.

" No German medical journal would allow me to publish my views, so I feel morally bound to write to you direct and tell you the straight truth. If the occasion arises, please do not hesitate to quote my letter in full."

Although the storm in the tea-cup continued for a while, the war-blinded were sensible enough to accept both contributions, and the money was used to found an institute for the blind. Munthe himself wrote a charming letter to the German war-blinded, for whom he felt a special sympathy.

In 1930 the English publisher raised the question of a reprint of Munthe's war book. Before agreeing, however, Munthe insisted on writing a new preface, which I quote in full:

" I have consented after some hesitation to a reprint of this little book. It was written in difficult circumstances and in a frame of mind unsuitable for literary effort; it was written *sur pied de guerre* in every sense of the word; it was written in pain and in anger. Anger is legitimate, it is even sacred. Anger has shone even in the eyes of Our Lord. Anger is necessary to man; it renders him temporarily insensitive and helps him to face sufferings and horrors he could never have endured when his head was cool. If we may believe good old Martin Luther it can even help a man to become a good writer and a good Christian: ' When I am angry I write well and I pray well ', wrote the great German reformer.

" But anger is a dangerous anaesthetic; it makes a man see red; it can even make him delirious and turn him into a raving lunatic or a monster. Anger expressed in mere words falls short of its purpose—it is useless to talk while the hurricane sweeps over one's head; nobody can understand a word one says. The natural outlet for anger is violence. For this very reason anger cannot last; it is too costly; no man can afford to be angry for long. Nor can a nation. England can hit hard, but her sons have never forgotten the rule of the games they played when they were boys; they are the first to come forth to shake hands when the contest is over. But it is easier to forgive than to forget.

" Should we forget? Christ told us to forgive our enemies, but He never told us to forget our dead. Can the dead forget, have our dead forgotten? We shall never know. But I know that I cannot forget what I have seen and felt as long as my heart beats, and the heart is the last to remember. I cannot even retract what I have written in this terrible book unless I lie to myself, for I wrote the truth as I saw it then with flaming eyes and bleeding heart. But I could not write such a book as this today. I am not the same man and I thank God for it. The storm has abated; the thunder and lightning has ceased; the vision has become clearer, the horizon has widened, there is room for understanding. Victors and vanquished, slayers and slain have become the same people struck blind by the wrath of God, unconscious and irresponsible, mere blood-dripping tools in the hand of Destiny. Now, when at last the curtain has gone down over the titanic tragedy, all that remains in the onlooker's mind is awe and pity."

Later, about 1933, Munthe agreed to have the book withdrawn from publication.

Perhaps his anger was fundamentally directed not so much against Germany as against war in itself: his book so often expresses genuine sympathy for the German wounded. One might go so far as to say that the real hero of the story is the young Bavarian soldier, who tears the dressing off his wound and bleeds to death to save the enemy doctor from falling into the Allies' hands.

In the Foreword to the first edition he wrote:

" Now and then I tried to say to myself that I disliked these dying Boches, but I cannot honestly say I did; in fact, I rather liked them. They were all so forlorn, so patient, so humble, so grateful for the little one was able to do for them. They were all delighted to come across a man who knew their language—those who could smile grinned all over with joyous surprise, those who could not, greeted the familiar sound with a friendly look or a tear in their tired eyes. Those who could speak, or nearly all of them, spoke with humiliation and shame of what they had witnessed and what they had done. They certainly did not spare themselves; on the contrary, they seemed to like to talk of their evil deeds as if it gave them some relief—in fact, they did not want to talk of anything else. I saw several of these men die. They died as brave men die."

Munthe is full of praise for the ordinary German private soldier, whom he depicts merely as over-docile and a victim of early training in blind obedience. To him the real " villains of the piece " are the German officers, one of whom, a Potsdam Guards' officer, he caricatures in the best *Simplizissimus* style. It is not surprising that this stereotyped caricature of the typical German Junker and militarist as a chinless, monocle-wearing half-wit, which was first started in Germany itself, should be mistaken abroad for the real thing, especially in time of war.

Human Contacts

MUNTHE DID NOT RATE HUMAN BEINGS AS A WHOLE very high, but he was tolerant and human almost to excess. "Judge not that ye be not judged" might be said to have been the guiding principle of his life. In particular the naïve assurance with which small-scale rogues set about their acts of fraudulence appealed to the strain of ironical kindness which was his to a marked degree. These shady customers may have interested him as psychological studies, but it was above all his deep sense of humanity which made the commandment "Judge not" a ruling factor in his life.

It was not only curiosity and adventurousness which prompted him in his youth to beard the notorious Sicilian bandit chief Leone in his lair; it was a desire to understand the mentality of outlaws and crooks as well as of the law-abiding.

His instinct to help and protect those who had wandered from the straight and narrow path sometimes brought him strange experiences.

Once, for instance, a man whom he had helped appealed to him a second time to get him off a prison sentence for timber stealing. On the first occasion Munthe had got his sentence curtailed and it was hoped that this would have reformed him and kept him straight. But to the Doctor's surprise his gaolbird friend reappeared after a few months and told his patron that he had been imprisoned again for theft; at first, he said, he had not had too bad a time; he had made friends with one of the warders, a kindly soul, who had often allowed him to leave the prison at night, an indulgence he had exploited to make several profitable deals, of which he had given a share to the warder. But now someone had informed on him, and he had come to Munthe to ask for money to help him escape.

The Doctor found these partial disclosures rather alarming, and told his protégé that he would have to look into the matter himself. The police then told him an astonishing story. His protégé and the warder had been in league together; he and a fellow-gaolbird had walked out of the prison together at night, got hold of the mail-bag brought by the steamer to Capri, and, helped by a literate fellow conspirator, purloined everything of value in it. Working by the light of the moon they had destroyed all the letters which contained no money, closed the mail-bag again, now emptied of swag, and dragged it back into its place. But the disappearance of so many letters, and above all of consignments of jewellery, had led to an enquiry and finally to the arrest and imprisonment of the innocent postal official; this had naturally delighted the real thieves, who believed that they were safe and that the police were on the wrong trail. But finally the police themselves began to have doubts, and now appeared to be on the track of the real criminals. This was too much even for Munthe. He told his friend point blank that this time he would not help him.

Not long after, however, his ex-protégé called on him again, this time decked out in a smart uniform and wearing the Fascist badge *Sempre Pronti*. And now it was he who was prepared to offer Munthe his protection.

*   *   *

The people of Capri well knew the Doctor's charitable nature, but he also had other fads and fancies which they occasionally exploited.

They knew, for instance, that he had a passion for preserving trees, especially oak trees. Capri is rich in tall trees, entirely thanks to Munthe, who paid yearly rents to various land-owners to prevent the trees on their estates being cut down and used as firewood before they had attained their full height. Today many of these trees have become landmarks on the island and are under Government protection as *Monumenti Nationali*. The two pines which border the path to San Michele are good examples.

The northern oak is not suited to the dry Capri summer. Nevertheless Munthe was especially fond of oaks; they were so rare in Capri, gave such welcome shade and, above all, were native to his country. There was one particularly beautiful oak which Munthe used to pass almost every day on his walks. It was on a private estate below the Queen's villa in the little ravine which separates the village of Ana-capri from Materita. A certain notorious Anacapri spiv and moocher one day thought out a way of making money out of this tree. Knowing the Doctor's habit of walking past it nearly every day about midday he decided to stand by it with an axe in his hand and hope for the best. Seeing the Doctor approach, the spiv quickly threw off his coat, rolled up his shirt sleeves and seized hold of the axe, which he had hired for the afternoon.

Munthe was surprised to see him standing by the tree, clutching the axe, and asked him what he was doing there. The man replied that he was penniless and about to fell the oak for firewood.

The Doctor retorted:

"You know, don't you, that the oak doesn't belong to you. I shall report you; you've got a bad enough record as it is; I'll get you deported here and now and sent miles away from the island."

The spiv was quite taken aback and cried out:

" That'll cost you a lot of money and lawyers' fees. Whereas for half a lire I can send you very much further still, somewhere from where there's no return."

This outburst of rage at first left Munthe entirely unmoved, and he started to walk on. But, his curiosity suddenly aroused, he turned back and asked the man to repeat what he had said, and what he needed the half lire for.

" A sharp little stiletto costs half a lire; one stab in the ribs with that would finish you; you'd never come back to Capri again!"

Munthe pretended to take the man seriously. Then, with a smile on his face, he calmly asked his would-be murderer what he expected to get for an oak like that. The rogue replied: " Fifty lire."

The Doctor stared up for a moment at the oak's green foliage, lost in thought. Then he looked down again at the wretched figure leaning against the trunk, gripping his axe and watching him, his eyes ablaze with hate. Finally, taking out his pocket book, he said calmly:

" Here's fifty lire for you, and—oh yes, another half lire for the knife."

For a moment the thief was speechless. Then it dawned on him that the *Signore* was not so easily bluffed, and that he was in fact quite different from what he had imagined.

*   *   *

One set of people, however, Munthe could never bring himself to trust, and they were lawyers. More than likely he had had unpleasant encounters with them at some stage of his life, for he maintained that their judgments were far from infallible, that they tended to complicate the simplest matters and to prolong law suits in their own interests. For years he had managed to avoid having to deal with them, but once he had to consult them about acquiring a piece of land.

Quibbles arose by the score, until Munthe lost patience and, to get the thing settled quicker, invited the lawyer who was dealing with the case to come on his yacht to Sorrento and beard the department concerned with him. There was a storm raging in the gulf, but Munthe was a good seaman and not at all alarmed.

When they reached the open sea the lawyer realized what he had let himself in for, and implored the Doctor to turn back. Munthe, of course, refused, and the terrified representative of justice at once began to regret all his previous high-handedness. Indeed, almost going down on his knees, he promised that if Munthe put him ashore alive he would get the whole affair settled at once. When they finally anchored in Sorrento the lawyer, pale but still alive, got the deal satisfactorily signed, sealed and delivered that very day.

But there was one lawyer in Capri, Roberto Serena, for whom the Doctor had always had the greatest respect. He used to say of him that not only was he clever—nearly all Italians are cleverer than North Europeans, especially in business—but that he was absolutely straight—in other words a gentleman.

At about the time of the land deal Munthe was in constant conclave with Serena in a protracted law suit against a lady who had persuaded the Doctor, much against his will, to allow her to rent San Michele, and who was now proving a most difficult tenant. At one of these sessions the opposing solicitor tried to calm the Doctor, whose temper was rising, by saying: "Do remember I'm your friend!"

"On the contrary," retorted Munthe, "I have only one friend in the legal profession, Roberto Serena."

Munthe had no use for the lady's eccentricities and was naturally annoyed at her refusal to leave San Michele, which she had only rented for a short time, and which, moreover, she wanted to refurnish and redecorate according to her theatrical taste. But he was too chivalrous to have her evicted by force. Instead he sent Serena to visit the celebrated beauty, whom d'Annunzio and Maurice Dekobra have immortalized in verse, and try to negotiate with her. Serena returned with his mission unfulfilled, but with such a glowing account of his hostess that the Doctor declared that he had obviously fallen in love with her.

"Me!" protested Roberto, "I should have said it was you! Anyone but you would have put the police on to her!"

A long story was attached to this letting of San Michele. The lady was one of the loveliest and most capricious women of the time; she was conspicuous wherever she went, and had a remarkable flair for creating backgrounds for her beauty. She once appeared at a Venetian carnival as a dogeressa in a gondola shaded with peacock feathers, with gaudy parrots and a snow-white greyhound; then again she created a sensation by appearing at a fancy-dress ball as Cleopatra drawn in a chariot by handsome slaves. In fact she spent her time thinking out and arranging settings for which her imagination craved.

Her love of animals was the complete antithesis of Munthe's. She used dogs, monkeys, parrots, snakes, tortoises and even baby leopards as a background to her brilliant appearance. She would, for instance, go about with pretty little marmosets on her shoulders, chained to her with gold chains, or parade the streets with a tame panther on a lead. She once appeared at the races with an Italian greyhound dyed blue to match the feathers in her hat.

Munthe disapproved of this form of animal love as strongly as he did of zoos and menageries. He had first met her in Rome, and from the day of their meeting she was fired with the idea of spending some time in his house, San Michele. From the first Munthe was dead against this plan. One evening, however, his household came running to tell him that a lady had just arrived at the door with twenty trunks and six servants, one of them a negro, and was demanding immediate admittance. Munthe at first refused to let her in—in fact rumour has it that the beautiful creature spent a night of drenching rain in the garden with her retinue and luggage.

Finally, however, an agreement was reached, and she spent many subsequent years of her adventurous life in San Michele. Of course she and the Doctor had many conflicts and often got on each other's nerves. There is the well-known story of a portrait of her wearing only a panther-skin. Munthe was asked his opinion of the work; he and his tenant happening to be on bad terms at the time, he answered brusquely: " I know her naked soul, and that's enough."

Even this San Michele phase, which brought Munthe very little profit and a great deal of worry, finally ended, and many years later Munthe called on his erstwhile tenant, who was then living in loneliness in a small room in London. She had sold her live and stuffed animals, jewels and furniture, but was as witty, original and entertaining as ever. Munthe had long forgotten his old rancour and was now friendly and anxious to help her. He was far too tolerant even of weaknesses foreign to his nature ever to bear malice. There are many people alive today, some good, some less good, who can boast of having enjoyed Munthe's friendship, but hardly any who can truthfully claim his dislike.

Up to the end of his long life women continued to admire, rave about and even love Munthe. In fact it was often said that he owed his very reputation as a doctor to women. In the conversation between him and his friend Norstrom in *The Story of San Michele* he reveals the secret of his extra-ordinary power over the opposite sex. Norstrom says to him: " You're always surrounded by women; even my cook is in love with you." To which Munthe replies: " Women are much braver than us men; they bear suffering and death more stoically: they have more pity and less vanity. . . . On the whole I admire women much more than men, but I don't tell them so." He certainly never told them—in fact he made a point of never flattering women. He was always courteous and attentive to them, but could also give them his opinion "straight from the shoulder". During her short and rather unhappy marriage to a Swedish Prince, Maria Pawlowna was Munthe's patient for a time, and in her memoirs she describes him as a stern, harsh tyrant.

Munthe's advice to his friend Norstrom in his book to follow his example and "not to rate women too high" is good and true up to a point, but not entirely. Admirable as the recipe may be, not everyone can apply it with success. A man's charm is surely part of his whole make-up, and this can never be fully analysed. There is always something inexplicable behind it.

Munthe might open his heart about women as a whole, but he was always discreet about individuals. Indeed the secrecy which professional etiquette enjoined on him soon became second nature to him, and was observed in regard to all women. Any remarks of his which outside observers might have thought revealing were in fact not revealing at all. He could read the hearts of others quickly enough, but his own was padlocked and he alone possessed the key.

Munthe's attitude to love, in the sense of passion, was, one might say, that of a doctor and psychologist rather than that of a poet. In *The Story of San Michele* he remarks that love has a "short, flower-like existence". In men it dies a natural death after marriage; in women it often continues for ever in the form of a purely motherly affection for what one might call the "once glorified, now perished hero of her dreams". Some of Munthe's friends, especially happily married couples, would sometimes protest that his views on love and marriage were much too prejudiced and pessimistic. He would listen to them good humouredly, but never change his views.

A story is current of an episode which occurred during his first marriage, and which perhaps throws some light on that period of his life. Friends who knew him then say that the young and handsome Fru Munthe had very pretty, well-shaped legs, but that in those days of long, trailing skirts, custom forbade their owners to exhibit them in public. Fru Munthe could only display them by going for walks in the pouring rain; this she would sometimes do on purpose, much to her husband's disgust and disapproval.

One might deduce from this story that, for all his tolerance, Munthe still retained something of the Puritan which the out-and-out Swedish upbringing of those days had made of him. And yet a more important factor than any early parental influence was that his keen intelligence and scientific honesty would not admit of romanticism in any form. Munthe understood and admitted passion's individual components; the satisfaction of instinct, which, he maintained, was man's chief drive, and woman's, which, he declared, were " hero-worship " and the " mother " instinct; but he would not admit that they ever fused into a single whole. One might say that he judged by the ' appearance ', but that the ' essence ' escaped him; how, then, could he believe in its existence? He regarded love in its highest form as an enriching virtue, but believed that as yet very few were capable of this. He once said: " Love in its highest and rarest form is best depicted by the image of a mistress gazing at her lover in wide-eyed wonder, with her hand laid protectingly on his shoulder." He added that women alone were capable of such love.

As the years passed Munthe entertained many more guests in San Michele. When he was away himself he would often hand the house over for weeks at a time to friends and acquaintances. His English friends, Esme Howard and Lord Simon, for instance, stayed there on their own, as did Princess Mafalda and her husband, and a certain Prince Wolkonsky, whom the First World War had left destitute.

Once some of Munthe's friends brought a certain Polish painter to Materita, to inspect the house and its art treasures. Sienkiewicz' novel, *Quo Vadis*, had just appeared, and the Polish artist had done a series of enormous and rather crude oil paintings illustrating the various scenes of martyrdom described in the book, which he was exhibiting in some villa on the island. He had a very good opinion of himself, and thought Michelangelo was nothing to him. He treated Munthe with hearty condescension, blissfully unconscious of the irritation his loud bragging was causing his host.

At the end of the visit the guests happened to be standing by one of Materita's treasures, a lovely Greek bust, impressive in its serenity. Bramarbas, who seemed especially taken with it, coolly proposed that he should paint Munthe's portrait and be given the Greek bust as payment in kind. He had no doubt about his offer being accepted, and was startled when Munthe, turning to the others, said gravely: " How *can* a man like this be allowed to go about loose? He ought to be locked up." At this the guests said good-bye and departed.

Munthe had for a while also used the old watch-tower, La Guardia, originally built as a fortress against the Saracens, to shelter some of his strange protégés. One of La Guardia's inmates was a Moscow doctor's wife. Her second child had been born a freak, which the father, a man of science, had wished to destroy. But the mother's instincts had revolted, and she had fled the country with her elder child, who was normal, and the younger, a deformed cripple. After many ups and downs she had reached Italy, where she heard about Munthe and decided to seek his protection.

As a doctor Munthe felt bound to agree with the father. But the mother's tragedy touched his feelings as a man, and he at once housed her with her two children in La Guardia, where the wretched child, who was blind and defective, was fed and cared for by his elder brother. The idiot child was horrifying to look at. He lived till he was 19 but never learnt to speak and could only utter plaintive moans.

Later the Russian woman had a love-affair with one of her compatriots, who at that time used to land on the island in shoals, following in Gorki's wake. She had two more children by this man, and again Munthe came to the rescue and kept them for many years. The father of the second family would brazenly hand Munthe bills at regular intervals, actually daring to make scenes if Munthe ever presumed to query them.

The Doctor, in fact, sheltered countless people whom no one else would have bothered about—not even the officials whose business it was—and who could rightly have been described as no concern of his. Perhaps the community relied on him too much as a last resort in really hopeless cases. The islanders were often heard to say of him: " He actually gives money to the poor, which shows how rich he must be." None of them stopped to think how very little he ever spent on himself.

He was always discreet in helping those whom others would have described as " too far gone ". A certain Norwegian lady could testify to this. She and her husband had suffered a cruel loss in the death of their only son. The father had taken to the Capri wine bottle, given up working altogether and was on the verge of ruin. Munthe took him in hand, ordered him to return home, paid his fare for him and made a new man of him.

But he usually kept these acts of charity very dark. On occasion, however, he would jokingly refer to what he called his " rough-and-ready kindliness ". He always reminded one of a certain Frenchman who defined the compassion of the Saints as " both strong and gentle, with nothing in it of that childish dread of seeing others suffer ".

Munthe never quoted the Bible: but he always knew the answer to the question: " Who is our neighbour?"

" He who most needeth our help."

Sight and Insight

IT WAS SPECIALLY TRAGIC THAT, WITH ALL HIS TALENTS, abilities and powers of observation Axel Munthe, while still a mere youth, should have had to face the fact that he might at any time go blind. Even as a schoolboy he was very short-sighted. He had to wear spectacles to read, and his eyes were very sensitive to light. But though from a purely optical point of view his vision was always poor his mind's eye was exceptionally clear. His memory was definitely visual, and he managed to perceive and achieve very much more than most men with normal sight.

Walking with him through the fields and gardens of Capri made the surroundings seem lovelier and more significant, for he seemed to see hidden beauties everywhere. To him a weed which we call ' Queen Anne's lace ' would become a veritable Queen's mantilla. Or he might describe one of the many weather-worn limestone boulders at the roadside as having a "kindly but somewhat stupid expression". He had such a remarkable flair for arranging flowers that one might have thought he had learnt the art from a Japanese decorator. If people were struck by and admired one of his still-life flower-pieces he would make some flippant retort such as: " Did you think I'd stick them in the vase head downwards?"

He always maintained that a climbing rose-bush at his window was a far greater work of art than all Materita's treasures combined, and that it was a real miracle every spring to see the first light green vine shoots sprouting against the brown wooden poles.

Visiting museums or old curiosity shops with him was quite an experience. He would often visit museums to inspect some new acquisition or to feast his eyes on old favourites. It was moving to see the pleasure he got merely from looking at certain pictures. One might, for instance, be standing beside him gazing at a magnificent Guardi, when a few magic words from him would at once bring the banqueting-hall to life, and one could almost hear the concerto violins strike up their melody.

Once he stood and stared for some time in doubt at a marble bust of a Greek goddess, declaring at last that, for all its undeniable beauty, the bust lacked a certain quality of ethereal rapture, with which the Greek artists of old always managed to endow their sacred images. The expression of the mouth, in particular, was far too carnal. He was later proved right, for that particular portion of the bust turned out to be a subsequent addition, which no one at the time was aware of.

Munthe's friends were always puzzled to know how much he actually saw with his one eye and how much his mind's eye supplied, and how with his weak sight he always managed to find the essentials. It was as though he had discovered a direct access, a secret gate to the heart of things, so that round-about routes were spared him. He was as sure in his aim as a water-diviner, and his imagination enabled him to discover the most important elements and to combine them in that eloquent unity which he would always perceive in a work of art or an expression of nature.

Axel Munthe had beautiful eyes, unusually dark blue in colour. The fact that these eyes were threatened with blindness from an early age was a constant obsession. He was under fifty years old when one day, after an exhausting and important consultation at the Stockholm Court, he had a sudden and very painful detachment of the retina of one eye. The consultation, which had been held in Drottningholm, the King's summer palace, concerned one of the younger princes, who was seriously ill, and destined to die young. The King and Queen had returned to Stockholm in their coach and four, which the Queen used to drive herself. When they heard that Munthe was lying ill at Drottningholm, almost unconscious with pain, they drove back at once to fetch him away themselves.

Munthe then went straight off to Wiesbaden to see Pagenstecher, the greatest living eye-specialist at that time, but even he could do very little for him. Pagenstecher prescribed a month's rest in a dark room, but it was too late to save the sight of the eye affected. Moreover the blind eye gave Munthe more and more pain, and every external stimulus caused him agony. Yet in spite of this he did a whole year's war service as a doctor. He could not stand light of any kind, and gradually ophthalmia threatened to break out in his good eye.

It was not till about eight years later that, on the advice of Professor Katz in Karlsruhe, he allowed his blind eye to be removed. After the operation the nurses tried to put him to bed, but he astonished them by getting up and saying: " Please remember it wasn't my leg; it was my eye." He then walked into the private ward which had been reserved for him, unpacked the picnic-basket so familiar to all his friends, lit the spirit-lamp and insisted on making tea for himself and for the two nurses who had attended the operation. Then at last he allowed them to put him to bed, for now the pain from the operation was becoming too much for him.

After the healing Munthe had to wear a glass-eye. The optician chosen to manufacture this delicate work of art had to visit Munthe three times to get the colour exactly right. He swore that he had never seen such deep blue eyes before. When Munthe at last succeeded in fixing this glass-eye into its socket and could wear it with comfort he found a relief from the previous constant inflaming of his sound eye and, before returning to Materita, stayed on for a time in Karls-ruhe, where he had a great many friends. But soon even in this eye a cataract slowly began to form. Gradually a thicker and darker veil began to separate him from the out-side world. For a long time he would have nothing done about it, and the fear that an operation for cataract might bring on another detachment of the retina tormented him constantly and drove him to consult doctor after doctor.

Soon he could see hardly a glimmer of light, had to fumble his way about even in his own room and to be helped with the simplest daily functions, which to a man of his indepen-dence was extremely humiliating. At last he decided to risk the operation.

A Swedish oculist friend of his had advised him to consult Vienna's most famous ophthalmologist practising at that time. He wrote to his Viennese friends, Prince and Princess Batthiana, telling them of this plan, confident that they would do their best to help him, especially as the Prince was himself an oculist.

When everything had been settled and Munthe was about to set off for Vienna, the whole plan had to be cancelled owing to a new regulation issued by the Third Reich. Munthe, helpless as he was, had to have a companion on the journey. But the companion in question was unfortunately a German, and, to get from Germany into Austria, German citizens had to pay the German Government a thousand marks, a measure which hit Austrian economy badly and was intended to prepare her for the annexation. This particular man, who was merely helping Munthe to get to Vienna for an operation, was harmless enough. But he could get no exemption.

Munthe was then in Berlin; he had previously visited London to have thirteen teeth removed to prepare for the operation. In those days this was regarded as a safeguard against infection. Stoic that he was, Munthe accepted this somewhat drastic procedure as " all in the day's work ".

Meanwhile he had heard of another eye-surgeon, Professor Löhlein of Freiburg, so all seemed well again. Two Karlsruhe friends of Munthe's, the Countesses Andlau, were actually waiting at their front door to receive him, when at the last moment another piece of German officialdom spoiled everything: another surgeon was appointed to the Freiburg chair, and Löhlein was summoned to Berlin, where he explained with profuse apologies that he would need first to learn the " ins and outs " of his new clinic, and that this would take him a fortnight at least.

Now Munthe lost patience and almost heart as well. In a mood of deep depression he declared that Fate was against him, and that, though comparatively young, Providence had obviously ordained that he should never regain his sight. Poor blind man that he was, he was clearly destined to return to the solitude of his old tower.

Munthe and his companion had to return home by way of Switzerland, where at least there was one last hope in the shape of Professor Vogt, an exceptionally able ophthalmic surgeon. Munthe agreed to consult him on the way through. After his two previous disappointments his state of nervous tension on the journey to Zürich was almost unbearable, but after a short consultation Vogt said that he would take Munthe into his clinic the very next day and operate on him as soon as possible. This decision was to Munthe like a deliverance from Hell.

Munthe never forgot the weeks he spent in Zürich; in fact it was there that his luck turned again. Vogt's exceptionally sure and confident manner restored Munthe's mental balance. And the *Pension* Florhof, where he first stayed, small and old-fashioned, with its cosy old china stove and its landlord's genial welcome, was extraordinarily soothing to his nerves, frayed by all his previous setbacks and by the agitation of his travels across Europe.

Vogt's new patient was inclined to be recalcitrant, but he managed him extraordinarily well. The morning after his arrival Munthe walked up to the nursing-home run by nuns, where Vogt treated all his private patients, burst into his consulting room and began rather arbitrarily to rearrange it, opening all the windows to let in the autumn air, setting up his tea-kettle and lighting his pipe. Vogt, a blond giant of a man, then appeared himself and at once rebuked his patient with that characteristic faint trace of German Swiss accent in his voice. "Dr. Munthe," he said, "for the next fortnight I must be in complete charge here, and you must do what I tell you. After that we can be good friends again."

All apostles of Aesculapius are notoriously bad and cantankerous patients. This was definitely true of Munthe. In his student days in Paris he had done eye operations himself, so he knew exactly what was being done to him now. The moment he no longer felt Vogt's hand on his forehead he boldly opened his eye to see if he could see and cried out in delight: "I can see you quite clearly. I never knew you wore spectacles."

But he had chosen the most dangerous moment possible to open his eye; it might entirely spoil the effect of the operation and was therefore strictly forbidden. Munthe had heard and seen the word *verboten* so often in Germany that he maintained it was a purely German invention: this time, however, he realized its importance and obeyed it. "No, no," said Vogt, "you mayn't see yet; I'm going to bandage you now and have you put to bed."

Munthe now had to submit to a further indignity. To prevent him touching his eye accidentally his hands were tied fast to the bed. He protested strongly at first, but was comforted by hearing de Valera's comment when, as a recent patient in the same clinic, he had been subjected to the same treatment: "These bandages are child's play compared to the chains with which they fettered me in Ireland."

Vogt was soon able to pronounce the operation a success, and the news spread like wildfire. A stream of reporters and thousands of reply-paid telegrams demanding details had to be dealt with, a task made doubly difficult by Munthe's objection to any premature announcement and to any form of publicity. But it was remarkable that so many people of different nationalities should be interested in Munthe's welfare.

The reaction in Zürich itself was most moving. Young and old, rich and poor seemed to rejoice at the good news. Children called with flowers and congratulatory letters, and sprays of orchids arrived with no name on them. What struck one above all was the number of anonymous tributes he received: little home-made presents, concert tickets and varied trinkets. Munthe longed to thank all these well-wishers, but was often frustrated by their own desire to remain anonymous. However, he managed to track down a few, and on one occasion called personally on one of his humbler admirers and gave her an inscribed copy of his book.

Later he was allowed to go out every day for a short stroll. One day, happening to pass a fruit stall on one of the Limmat bridges, he noticed swarms of birds pecking at the hulled walnuts and the owner of the stall for some reason ignoring it. Munthe stopped by the stall, and the lady owner, a hand-some middle-aged Ticino woman, started chatting to him at once like an old acquaintance. "How d'you like Zürich, Doctor Munthe?" A few minutes' talk revealed that this simple peasant woman had read and admired *The Story of San Michele* in Italian. Shopkeepers would often refuse to charge him for what he bought. Time and again he would be recognized from old newspaper photographs, and the whole

[136]

population seemed to want him to share the produce of that glorious autumn of 1934.

By a curious coincidence the succession of obstacles with which Munthe had had to contend had resulted in the operation finally taking place on the feast day of St. Francis of Assisi, the patron saint and friend of animals and the poor. No one knew this, and Munthe, who had a particular affection for this saint, was amazed to discover engraved on a small silver box given him many years before by an ornithologist friend the date " 4.X., the feast of St. Francis ".

Apart from this Munthe never bothered about birthdays. He used to say that they had been " invented purely as an excuse for Kings and Queens to send each other telegrams ". And yet this one curious coincidence impressed him. One night during his early convalescence he had a dream. In the dream the Saint appeared to him, having also had an eye operation—which in those days meant having one's temples burned with red-hot irons—and bent over him with a benevolent smile on his face.

Later, in a letter which was published in *The Times* on December 7, 1934, Munthe described this dream:

" Ever since the day your great paper thought it worth while to tell its readers that I had undergone a successful operation in Zürich and had regained my sight, I have been receiving by every mail a large number of signed and unsigned letters of congratulation from your country. Since it is wholly impossible for me to answer personally all these letters, I venture to ask leave to trespass on your columns with these lines to express my deep gratitude for so much kindness. I did not know I had so many friends in England. I am under no illusion as to whom I have to thank for this friendship. I owe it all to our mutual friends the birds, so near the heart of every English man and woman, and so near my own. As I am writing these lines after weeks of anxious suspense, I begin to ask myself whether my indebtedness to our winged friends is not even far greater.

" The night after my operation was full of torment. I had been operated on by a master hand, but my fate was uncertain. My head was exhausted by insomnia, and my courage was beginning to flag, for man gets his courage during his sleep. My thoughts were as dark as the night around me; the night I well knew might never come to an end. Suddenly a ray of light flashed from my tired brain down to my very heart. I remembered all at once that it was the *giorno santo*, the anniversary of St. Francis of Assisi, the life-long friend who had never forsaken me in the hour of need. The day of St. Francis! I heard the fluttering of wings over my head and far, far away the soft, silvery chime of the bells I knew so well. The pale Umbrian saint, the friend of all forlorn creatures on this earth, stood by my side in his torn cassock, just as I had so often seen him on the frescoed walls of his dim chapel when my eyes could see. Swift-winged birds fluttered and sang around his head, others fed from his outstretched hands, others nestled fearlessly among the folds of his cassock.

" The fear that had haunted me so long left my tormented brain, and a wonderful stillness and peace fell over me. I knew I was safe. I knew that the Giver of light was having mercy on me and would let me see again His beautiful world.

" ' The day is breaking,' whispered the nurse."

Soon Munthe was allowed to take longer walks, and on these walks he made many new acquaintances. During his convalescence he was like a child rejoicing in a world that had been restored to him. So much had changed during his long period of blindness, and he took a new interest in everything; for one thing women had now taken to having their hair cut short and wore short skirts!

Vogt's face would beam with pleasure, and he would say: " Every morning when I wake up my first thought is: ' Axel Munthe—he's all right now!' "

When Munthe got his new spectacles he could actually read—for the first time for years!

Vogt would not hear of taking a fee, but was delighted with Munthe's present of an antique Swedish silver goblet engraved with the donor's thanks.

At last the day came when Munthe could continue his southward journey. As the train crossed the Alps he stood stock-still at the window admiring the snow-covered mountains, lakes and green valleys. But to the question: " What was the loveliest sight you saw today?" he replied at once: " The stars."

In Royal Circles

THOSE WHO DID NOT KNOW MUNTHE OR WHO KNEW HIM very slightly always attributed his connection with royalty to snobbishness. Partly as a joke against himself and yet with a certain smugness he would tell one that there was no royal residence in Europe where he had not spent at least one night. A remark like that was bound to put people's backs up, but he always qualified it by adding: " If you can possibly avoid it, never spend a night in a palace."

Munthe would certainly have been hard put to it to avoid spending his last years in the palace of Stockholm, which was, indeed, beautiful inside and out, but old-fashioned, uncomfortable and most unsuitable for an old man suffering from asthma. The King would certainly have been hurt if Munthe had refused, and might even have regarded it as *lèse-majesté*. He and the Doctor were almost contemporaries; Munthe had been the Queen's physician-in-ordinary and many recollections of years long past bound them together. True, they did not have much to say when they did meet, and the King's chief pleasures, shooting and tennis, bored Munthe. But King Gustaf really needed the Doctor's company, and insisted on his dining with him at least once a week. The two men had been friends for so long that their regard for each other was virtually taken for granted. Once, when one of Munthe's many schemes for a journey south had again fallen through (this time he had planned to fly from Stockholm to Rome), a friend asked him why even the King had been against it. Munthe replied: " Because he likes me." It was true enough. King Gustaf's reason for not wanting his friend to risk the strain of the air journey was not merely concern for his health, but a desire to keep him near him in Stockholm.

Munthe was usually very reserved about his friendship with the King, but he paid a very fine and frank tribute to it in his written contribution to the Commemorative works published on King Gustaf's seventy-fifth birthday. This is what he wrote:

" ' Have you seen the King?' was the old Laplander's first question as I sat down by the window of his smoky hut. ' Have you seen the King?'

" Yes, old Laplander, I can answer that question today. I have seen the King: I've seen him at close quarters for a whole life-time while I still had two eyes to see with. I knew him well. In fact the Queen Mother once said to me that I knew him better than most people. Those words coming from her lips mean something, for she was one of the wisest women I've ever met.

" For twenty-five years Sweden's King has lived among us, his people. No barriers of ceremonial or stilted etiquette have come between him and us. His bearing has been the same towards everyone, high and low, rich and poor. His life is a page in Sweden's history, an open book accessible to all. All can read it in the full light of day and follow his day-to-day record of upright, conscientious work for the betterment of his people, of wise and steady leadership in times of joy and suffering, and of fearless and memorable utterance in times of trouble.

" But I myself have also read another and quite different book, a closed book which only a few may glance at. I read it in the dim glow of a lamp beside a sick bed, and was profoundly moved; it is a noble human document that could never find expression in words, a reserved man's unwritten diary; page after page recording years of trial and tribulation, of hopes unfulfilled and helpless struggles against suffering and death. That book is the record of the lonely dweller in Stockholm Palace who, though bereaved, remained steadfast at his post in his empty home. Long dreary winters followed one another, bringing an endless stream of worries, disappointments and anxieties; shorter and shorter were the summers in which he saw his friends again, while even these were darkened by presentiments that all had been in vain.

" Until her strength gave out our Queen fought proudly for her life and her throne. She was a Queen indeed, and would not weaken. Though she continued to wear the crown, it became a crown of thorns which pierced her furrowed brow. In the end, exhausted by the hopeless struggle, even her courage began to fail. The burden of her cross, too, fell more and more on the shoulders of that other who, chivalrous and loyal, accompanied her on her long calvary, with words of comfort and understanding, until at last the Great Reaper came, who is more merciful than life.

" The dark clouds have dispersed. Evening approaches, but the sun is still high over the horizon. Dusk will not fall for many hours. New generations follow on, enlivening once more the old Royal Palace round the figure of the aged King, who still makes light of the years.

" Down below, in the Palace yard, the flags are dipped in salute, to the cheers of the populace. And all around, Sweden's people stand bare-headed in loyalty and allegiance to its King and in gratitude for a good night's watch at the helm of Sweden."

Though Munthe may have often breathed Court air this could never destroy in him the quality so rarely found outside palace confines, which Schiller calls " manly pride in face of kingly thrones ". He travelled from Court to Court, mixed freely

The Swedish Royal Family at Drottningholm Castle, 1909

*Queen Victoria of Sweden in mourning for her mother,
the Grand Duchess of Baden*

The Doctor, the monkey and the fox-terrier
An interior in San Michele

with Emperors and Kings and yet was never a courtier. The words of his friend Kipling are appropriate in his case:

"If you can talk with crowds and keep your virtue,
    Or walk with Kings—nor lose the common touch."

This he could do, and was therefore beloved by the high and mighty. He was always himself in any company, and had therefore something of value to offer these great ones of the earth, something they rarely encountered—a genuine and unprejudiced point of view. They knew they could always get the truth out of him, distasteful though it might be; they consequently trusted him and sought his advice on critical occasions.

And yet, after finally consenting to become the Queen of Sweden's physician-in-ordinary he did to some extent become a prisoner in Court circles. Like it or not, he subsequently found himself constantly meeting members of other reigning houses of Europe who were related to the King and Queen of Sweden either by blood or marriage. This, in fact, led to his meeting the Russian Czar and Czarina in 1913, when the Russian and Swedish Sovereigns met in Finland. Munthe, as the Queen's doctor, had travelled with her. The ceremonial did not, however, prevent him noticing almost at once that the Empress Alexandra really needed medical attention far more than his own Royal patient, who was at that time tolerably well; the Empress was literally obsessed by fears of assassination. Both Czar and Czarina wanted Munthe to come and settle in St. Petersburg if only for a short time. But the First World War prevented him from ever doing this. Munthe's friend and compatriot, Kurt Bonde, refers to this plan in his book *I Skuggan av San Michele*. He writes: "The world might have been different today if the Emperor and Empress had had Axel Munthe and not Rasputin to guide them at the time of Russia's collapse."

On another occasion Munthe was nearly caught up in the wheels of world history. But here we must look a little further afield.

Munthe had made great friends with Prince and Princess Max of Baden. A collection of photographs was taken during the long visit which the Prince and Princess paid to Capri—of summer days spent sailing and anchoring in various small harbours in the lovely Sorrento Gulf. The Prince later gave Munthe an album of these photographs, inscribed on the cover: " The Germans in Capri ", a joking reference to the well-known chapter in Munthe's *Memories and Vagaries*. Whenever they went ashore at any of the small, primitive, coastal villages the Prince and Princess had automatically cast off their incognito, and the Prince wrote under a photograph of himself and the Doctor: *I fratelli*—' the brothers ', which the local fisher-folk had always supposed them to be.

In the dark days of the German war collapse Prince Max, the ' Red Prince ', had a short period of office as Chancellor, the last before the Revolution. During the crisis he often longed to have his ' brother ' at his side to advise him, for once before in his life the latter had proved his best adviser. Who knows, things might have turned out differently if the Prince had had the Doctor's support in his country's crisis! But it was probably then too late to apply the remedy against collapse and revolution which Munthe in later days declared to have been appropriate: Prince Max, he said, should himself have donned his silver helmet, ridden down the *Unter den Linden* and persuaded the people that their duty was to save Germany from collapse and work for tolerable peace terms.

But Prince Max would probably not have followed this advice at the time, the crisis being too grave and he himself not a strong enough man. The cruel disillusionment felt by all classes in Germany after so many years of effort had given way to a paralysing indecision. Only a man of exceptional genius and courage could have warded off the inevitable, and at that fateful hour no such man appeared.

Nevertheless Munthe's verdict on Germany's fate in 1918 is in itself interesting. In his youth he had been a rabid radical and anti-monarchist and, moreover, in the 1914-18 war, a passionate supporter of the Entente. He was far from advocating autocratic rule, but being in his maturity a man of strong and independent character, he regarded the courage to shoulder responsibility as man's highest duty, especially in those dark days of stress, when the passions of an unbridled mob had to be quelled.

His judgment was probably sound from a purely academic point of view, but his notion of a noble knight arising to slay the wicked dragon was pure fantasy; he had no true conception of the dragon's power.

Unfortunately the Prince was ill during his short period of office and therefore even less competent to stem the course of events. With the best and soundest intentions he had to bow to the inevitable. Surrounded as he was by waverers, he could not screw himself up to take the plunge on his own.

Munthe's capacity to act alone stood the test once again when the Queen was lying in Stockholm Palace so desperately ill that the doctors attending her pronounced her condition hopeless. As a last resort the King decided to summon Munthe from England. For weeks the Queen had been forbidden to sit up in bed, but Munthe now persuaded her to get up and sit in a chair, where she could breathe more freely.

Provisional arrangements for the Queen's funeral and subsequent rites had already been made. Munthe, however, insisted instead that Her Majesty should make a trip to the south in the Royal train; this, he declared, was not only possible but essential. Professor Krehl of Heidelberg, whom he had called in as a second opinion, agreed with and approved both his diagnosis and treatment.

On the first night in the train the Queen slept well, and the next morning Munthe, Krehl and de Geer, the Groom of the Chambers, were in high spirits and went for a walk through the old town of Lübeck, while the train was shunted on to a siding in the station. They then travelled on to Rome, where the Queen lived another four years in the Villa Svezia.

It is harder for royalties than for ordinary people to distinguish true affection and loyalty from the mere display of it. And one can see why so many Kings and Queens took Axel Munthe to their hearts. He was so firmly planted in his own distinguished world that merit alone could impress him. An incident which occurred once in Solliden, one of the Queen's summer residences, illustrates this well. Munthe was there with the rest of the Court, when one day the Court photographer asked the King's leave to take a few photographs. The King sent for Munthe, who happened to be strolling in the park, to come and be photographed with him. The Doctor at first refused; then, to goad him, the King said: " Come on, you're in quite distinguished company, you know!" To which Munthe replied: " So are you."

The Queen's life in Capri was entirely simple and informal. She loved going for walks with Munthe and his dogs and her own poodle, or having tea in some solitary spot in Anacapri. On these walks she always wore what the islanders wore, plain plaited straw sandals and dresses made of white Capri wool. Her suite and the detective were told to keep as much as possible out of sight.

The lady-in-waiting, Countess Taube, did not share her mistress's *penchant* for precipitous climbs up narrow, stony ravines; in fact once, when her exquisite shoes had been ruined by this rough usage, she said despairingly to a young German, whom the Queen had invited to join them on their walk: " Oh, why does Her Majesty insist on climbing up these gutters?"

Munthe used to visit his patient every day in Casa Caprile, the villa which was eventually built for her under his supervision. Many difficulties had arisen during the process of building. For instance, a wily fellow, whose property bordered on the site of the Queen's villa, suddenly announced his intention of starting a pig-farm on that very spot, declaring, however, that he would renounce his plan entirely and sell the piece of land to the Queen, at the same time quoting a fabulous price for his ' altruism '. There was nothing for it—the piece of land had to be bought. And on it the Doctor built the miniature Villa Sole, which has since passed through many hands, but today belongs to his son.

In those days Casa Caprile had very primitive approaches. The village sewer flowed along one of the garden walls; it was open, full of dead cats and other refuse, and stank horribly. Again the Doctor had to fight hard to get this business settled. Even after all these improvements and in spite of its magnificent position looking eastward towards Monte Solaro, Capri's highest mountain, and westward over olive groves and across the sea as far as Ischia, Casa Caprile was not to everyone's taste. Under the pseudonym of ' Mr. G.' the King once visited the Queen there. Unfortunately he happened to slip up on the wet, jagged stones and fall flat on the ground, much to the village boys' delight, and that one visit was enough for him.

Once the Queen was in such a weak state that she was forbidden to climb any steps. Her return to Sweden was long overdue and a Swedish ship was anchored in the harbour, waiting to take her back. But she could not climb the companionway from the swaying pinnace on to the ship's deck (at that time the *Grande Marina* had no jetty). On this occasion, too, Munthe had to come to the rescue. He summoned his friend, Police Commissioner Vacca, to his aid, and the two decided that Vacca, armed with a letter from Munthe to the Admiralty in Naples, should scour the bay for the most suitable Italian vessel and charter it. Luckily Vacca soon returned with a suitable boat provided with a wooden superstructure, which enabled the Queen to board the ship quite comfortably.

When he tells that story Vacca always adds: " I saw that the Doctor was really pleased with me that day. He put his hand on my shoulder and said, ' I knew you wouldn't fail me.' For once he didn't even comment on my tie, though he usually made a point of criticizing it, saying it was ' too loud '."

Munthe would often accompany the Queen to Karlsruhe. The palace there was small and looked like a Spitzweg painting. Munthe liked it on the whole, though the importance which the Queen's parents, the Archduke and Duchess of Baden, attached to questions of rank and etiquette sometimes amused him: and he made fun of the strict order of precedence maintained at Court dinner parties. He himself insisted from the start on being excused from this silly ceremonial, and at first amazed the Karlsruhe public by his uncouth behaviour in jumping off the running-board of the coach as the Royal train drew into the station, totally ignoring the red carpet specially laid down and striding off with his dogs, while everyone else stood respectfully in line waiting for the Queen to alight.

The Archduke and Duchess of Baden soon took the Doctor to their hearts, and treated him as a friend, exempting him from the usual Court formalities. Munthe was much attached to the kindly and courteous old Archduke; he would talk about him for hours, comparing him to ' Old King Cole ' in the setting of his peaceful little duchy. The Archduke, for his part, always addressed Munthe as "mon cher", and this soon became his nickname at the Court of Baden.

The Archduchess was a Hohenzollern and the Emperor Frederick's sister. Energetic to a degree, she was ebullient by nature and tireless in her devotion to duty. Her chief interest was founding charitable organizations, and Heads of schools and hospitals rather dreaded her periodic tours of inspection, for she was quick to notice imperfections.

This dominating lady often differed from the Queen's physician-in-ordinary about her daughter's medical treatment. In spite of their mutual esteem these two domineering natures fell out from time to time, for in medical matters, as indeed in everything, Munthe was always downright and adamant; and many were the scenes that he had with the old lady, much to the astonishment of her suite, who had never yet known any-one even dare contradict her. Once when the Queen was seriously ill with a high temperature Munthe forbade anyone to visit her and instructed her nurses to bar the door of the sickroom even against her mother, the Archduchess. The Archduchess gave way, but it was long before she forgave the Doctor or could find a good word to say for him.

But Munthe later witnessed the collapse of all this stagey Court ceremonial, upon which his attitude towards the Arch-ducal family changed entirely, and in a manner very typical of him. It was his first visit to the Baden *Residenz* after the revolution, and his host this time was his personal friend, Prince Max of Baden. The old Grand Duchess was now a widow and had experienced all the terror of Germany's collapse. In the early stages of the revolution they had had to rescue her through an attic window and take her away to safety while the crowds were storming the palace.

Soon after he arrived Munthe asked Prince Max to lend him a frock-coat, a thing which he had never in his life possessed and had often made fun of. To him it symbolized the grave solemnity of those " Priviest of Privy Councillors ", a type now extinct. How often he had seen those frock-coated figures at Court receptions standing stiffly and silently, waiting for the guests to arrive! He used to say that they reminded him of black storks, and was surprised not to see them standing on one leg. The Prince was therefore naturally intrigued at this sudden *volte-face*, and thought it must be a joke on his guest's part. But it was far from that. Munthe quickly explained that, now that the Archduchess was a lonely old woman, dethroned, impoverished and with no suite, he wanted to pay her his respects in the old-established fashion. He who alone had despised ceremonial in the old days, now wanted to conform to it meticulously.

Among his patients were several Royal princesses, who had had tragic lives and died dramatic deaths. Three of these were murdered: the Empress Alexandra of Russia, her sister, Princess Sergius and the Empress Elizabeth of Austria. He also visited the Empress Eugénie in Paris when she was an old woman—in fact she presented him with a large, grey pearl, which he wore constantly up to the day of his death.

The exquisitely lovely Elizabeth of Austria was so enchanted with San Michele that she wanted to buy it herself. Many a time did Munthe and she sit together in the loggia, gazing down at the blue gulf. Once he actually wrote to her to ask her to help a Danish sculptor, whom he had found in Rome almost starving. This particular case worried him day and night. One day he visited the sculptor's dingy studio and laid a death mask of Heinrich Heine and a copy of his " Book of Songs " on the table, intending them to act as a stimulus to the sculptor to do a bust of Heine. The inspiration behind this was Munthe's own passion for Heine and his *Lieder*, which he loved to sing himself.

For two whole months the Danish sculptor shut himself up in his studio, and then one day, quite unexpectedly, invited the

Doctor to come up and inspect his work. In the two months he had completed a full length statue of the poet, leaning back in an armchair, his head slightly to one side, his eyes half-closed, as though sunk in thought.

The Empress Elizabeth, who shared Munthe's admiration for Heine, bought the statue, and had a marble copy made, which she set up in the park of the Achilleion, her castle in Corfu. When the German Emperor later bought the property he had the statue removed. It subsequently found its way to Hamburg.[1]

[1] The sculptor was Hasselries. During the time of the "Third Reich" the statue disappeared and is now apparently in France, somewhere near Toulon.

The Man

Axel Munthe was one of the many to whom the well-known saying attributed to one of the Fathers of the Church is particularly applicable, that " the human soul is by nature Christian ".

Munthe was Christ-like in feeling and action, although his keen intellect prevented him believing in the Church's traditional doctrine of salvation. Darwin's materialist theories, which in his youth prevailed everywhere, especially in France, demanded that man should manage " without the hypothesis " of a Divine creation and world order, and, indeed, claimed that the theory of evolution would in the end explain the origin of life wholly in terms of cause and effect. Moreover, Munthe as a man would have considered it unworthy to regulate his conduct in this world with a view to reward in the next.

One is reminded here of the main character, Dr. Rieux, in Camus's novel *The Plague,* who cannot himself explain his life of selfless devotion to his fellow-men. He does not believe in a Divine order, and yet acts as though he did, in complete contradiction to so many believers, who do just the opposite.

" But," he says, " as death ultimately rules the world, it is perhaps better for God's sake, even though one may not believe in Him, to wage war against death and not trouble about Heaven, which leaves us for ever in doubt."

" Yes," agrees Tarron, the Doctor's friend. " I see what you mean. But your victories can only be temporary."

" I know. But that's no reason for giving up the fight."

[152]

" What's taught you all that, Doctor?"

Without a moment's thought the Doctor replied:

" Suffering."

Dr. Rieux and Munthe certainly had much in common; Munthe would, however, have probably been less outspoken. For his part he refused to have his wits dulled in any way, even by belief, just as he would refuse all narcotics before an operation, however much he might dread the pain. He had seen too many cases of people to whom belief was a mere anaesthetic, a drug which sheltered them from life and death. He wanted to endure these without such help, but took care not to exact from others what he was prepared to enjoin on himself. He left them tranquil in their beliefs, and never refused to ease their bodily pains with narcotics.

The thought of death obsessed him all his life. It seemed to be ever-present in his mind, as in primitive banquets and sacrificial ceremonies, where it was represented symbolically. This *ideé fixe* had made him place above his dining-room door in San Michele a small mosaic representing a skeleton holding wine-jars in each hand. The figure of Death, holding in its hands the wine of life and all its pleasures, was meant as an exhortation to joy, and to the principle of *Carpe Diem*. Live for the day, give your lives meaning and value! The wine in the grim skeleton's hands is a symbol of this, an offering on life's altar, teaching one not merely to exist but to live.

Bernanos makes an old priest say: " The heathens were wiser about their gods. They somehow always managed to delude this wretched world into believing that it was linked with the Invisible through their Pantheistic conception."

This was roughly Munthe's attitude to death and its manifold symbols. He also possessed a delicately carved ivory skull, about the size of a walnut, which up to his death he would often take down and gaze at for hours, lost in thought.

He longed above all to be able to believe in the continuation of personality, and the survival of the individual after death. In fact he was always harping on it as though he yearned to have his doubts removed, and envied people who had none. For him it always remained the *Ignorabimus* of an honest, resigned scepticism. Sometimes he would even quote the passage in Renan: "Tout est possible—même Dieu." He said at times: "If only I had the right childlike faith!" A friend once asked him if he had ever had it, to which he replied: " It sounds absurd, but I've never had time."

But this scepticism was not a symptom of disillusioned old age; far from it; in his case the eternal problem always stirred in him new fantasies and possibilities. Sun and nature worshipper that he was, he had been known in his happy and expansive moods to extol life's beauty with a heart full of gratitude. Life seemed to play on his soul like a glorious symphony, in keys ranging from sad minor to jubilant major.

He devoured the works of Schopenhauer, but something in him revolted against Schopenhauer's pessimism. The problem of immortality was always uppermost in his thoughts, and once he actually promised to hand over Materita, lock, stock and barrel, to a guest who was staying there if he or she could convince him on the question of personal survival. The guest later reported their talk, adding with a laugh: " I tried my best but never got Materita!"

Munthe hated being asked his age, and his counter to outside pesterers was always: " I reached a thousand some hundreds of years ago." Occasionally he would say half jokingly: " I wonder which of my contemporaries will outlive me", and always backed Bernard Shaw and King Gustaf, the latter because he was by nature calm, and a good sleeper; he always compared him to an engine which ran on very little fuel.

The last time Munthe met Jacob von Uexküll, the biologist, was in June 1943, on the little steamer on which Munthe left Capri for the last time. When the Doctor again started on his favourite subject about the immortality of the soul, Uexküll retorted in his usual cheerful way: " Well, we're both approaching this transition stage now, and if by chance we meet on the other side you'll have to admit that my faith in what Goethe calls ' higher spheres of purer activity ' was justified."

★   ★   ★

Long before the days of poetry albums it was the fashion to offer one's friends a questionnaire, which they had to answer truthfully—a form of confessional practised as a game. In England these books were called " Confession Books ". Axel Munthe once consented to answer one of these, which he did as follows:

1. What human quality do you rate the highest?
—Courage.
2. What faults do you find it easiest to forgive?
—All.
3. What quality best helps a man to get on?
—Brazenness.
4. What do you regard as life's greatest boon?
—Sudden death, with no doctors anywhere about.
5. What would you miss most in life?
—A sense of humour.
6. What do you think of the trend of present-day Western Civilization?
—If its aim is purely materialistic then it's on the wrong track.
7. What do you consider the most important invention in the history of man?
—Wine, Leonardo da Vinci's *divino liquore*.
8. Do you belong to any religious denomination? If so, which?
—I believe in God, but doubt the soul's immortality.

9. What do you consider the first essential of a happy marriage?

—The capacity to forgive.

10. What historical figure do you admire the most, and why?

—St. Francis of Assisi.

11. What classic work of art has impressed you most?

—The Parthenon frieze.

12. Name five of your favourite books.

—The Bible, Dante, Shakespeare, Cervantes and Goethe.

13. What are your favourite flowers?

—Lilies of the valley.

14. What is your favourite colour?

—Sky-blue.

15. What is your favourite animal?

—My old dog.

16. What is your favourite exercise?

—Walking.

17. What weather and season of the year do you like best?

—The spring.

18. What is your favourite food and drink?

—Apples, cranberries and wine produced from my own vineyards.

19. What is your favourite recreation?

—Humming Schubert to myself.

20. What is your motto in life?

—Live dangerously, and trust life.

*   *   *

It is relevant at this point to record the meditations of a priest, Peter Lippert, who had just read *The Story of San Michele* and was intrigued both by the book and its author. Here are certain points which he noted down.

" ' It was a lovely day ' writes Axel Munthe, reminiscing

on his past life. This twilight admission strikes a cheerful, nostalgic note, and makes one long to know more about the life of such a man.

" *The Story of San Michele* is actually a modern example of a devotional work, but only for those who can read between the lines.

" And even if some of the book were untrue, if it were merely a piece of ironical fiction, the stories the author tells form a true and genuine picture of humanity.

" He can even be lenient towards the absurdities of his fellow men, and, indeed, his own, for his knowledge gives him both wisdom and sympathy. One can truly say of the book: ' This spring water is both clear and cold. But it tastes like bitter tears.'

" He could not even find words to express his charitable feelings towards all this world's creatures, because he himself hardly realized the essential goodness of this charity.

" The passage in which he describes the saints in Paradise as themselves forgetting the good they did on earth is very typical of him. He believes that each remembers only his fellow-saints' good deeds, and that the sum total of their works is known to God alone.

" This goodness is a clever goodness free of illusion, and therefore also always tinged with irony. It is not introspective and demands no set performances but flows easily and cheerfully over the inner basins of the soul, as Roman fountains do. It does not pause to think what the reward will be, thanks or abuse.

" Goodness such as this is not the pale product of calculation, but is essentially a grace—a vocation from above. But of course grace does not function mechanically, nor, as an engine, can it peter out. Grace needs co-operation and an infinite awareness. Axel Munthe possessed this awareness, this tough will to co-operate.

" And at the same time he often criticized himself relent-lessly—one might say cruelly—though this criticism usually took the light, amusing literary form of dialogues with doubles, ghosts, demons or jolly hobgoblins. Perhaps God grants his special grace only to those anxious to receive it, and to those whom he sees running out to meet Him.

" But Munthe was certainly not religious in the generally accepted sense, and he certainly did not belong to any special denomination. And yet he possessed what many, who seem to have nothing except religion and therefore get no real benefit from that religion, have not got—he possessed in its original, elemental goodness the foundation stone which is the basis of all true godliness: reverence, understanding and altruism. 'One has no right to hoard money for oneself. Every penny you hoard you will lose, and every penny you give away is yours for ever. Money belongs to no one in this world—it's the property of the devil. . . .'

" Only simple people will accept charity from others without shame. The more complex, alert and aware—one might almost say the more cunning—people are, the more complicated is their attitude to charity. Indeed where even charity fails, the strength of God's love is itself defeated, and He can only exert His omnipotence. And God's omnipo-tence without his special Grace—is Hell.

" But the angels we send forth from our souls which hunger to understand bring with them from their journey-ings all earthly creatures, and even their creator, and lead them into our midst. And the more of these often dubious characters we shelter from life's highways and byways, the livelier our life's marriage feast becomes. And then . . . it was a lovely day."

...nthe's house at Leksand

...n and Malcolm Munthe in the garden, 1947

Axel Munthe in Stockholm

King Gustaf of Sweden and Axel Munthe

FAME

" I want no write-ups about me in the papers after my death—just a plain announcement." This was how the Doctor would deal with reporters who kept calling on him, expecting that he would be flattered by their attentions.

Munthe had admirers all over the world, who longed to meet him. The Capri cab-drivers knew this only too well; they would show their fares the ordinary sights of the island and then, in the hope of getting extra tips, keep their eyes skinned for a glimpse of the celebrated Dr. Munthe, who at that time was often to be seen walking along the main road from Capri to Anacapri. As Munthe was never known to hire a cab himself and the drivers all agreed that he must have a special brand of leg, their only way of making money out of him was by showing him off to their other fares.

If they were lucky they would catch a glimpse of a tall thin figure striding along ahead of them. They would then quickly point him out to their fares, whip their horses into a trot and pull them up with a jerk when they caught up with him.

On one occasion two hysterical Englishwomen sprang out of one of these cabs and rushed at Munthe merely to tell him how they worshipped him and how blissfully happy they were to have met him at last.

Munthe replied politely but gravely:

" You are mistaken. I'm afraid I must disillusion you. Axel Munthe is dead."

Highly embarrassed, the ladies apologized, while the Doctor walked on, smiling to himself. But on the following day he was caught out. The English ladies, who had meanwhile made inquiries, lay in wait for him and rushed at him again, this time shaking their fists at him and shouting:

" You wicked man! We've been crying all night. But this time you can't fool us. You *are* Axel Munthe!"

This time Munthe shook them both warmly by the hand and said:

"Well, you may be right. Perhaps I am."

A certain journalist had a somewhat similar experience on the piazza. Someone tipped him a wink, and he trailed the Doctor as he strolled along arm-in-arm with his friend Doctor Prozillo. Catching up with him the reporter whipped out his camera. But the Doctor stepped quickly back with an assumed air of modesty, pointed to Prozillo, and said:

"This gentleman's the famous writer and celebrity; he's the man you're after, not me."

Prozillo stepped nobly into the breach and posed patiently while the hoodwinked reporter snapped him.

On one occasion Munthe said: "I'm made for life; I've had a marvellous offer to tour all the large American cities. I shall accept provided that wherever we go I shall be allowed to sit in a cage on the stage. I shall also insist on having a notice board fixed to the bars: 'No teasing or feeding', and a keeper to take me round and give short lectures about me whenever we're on show. But I fancy one show will be enough for them, and the promoters will be glad enough to call the tour off."

The phenomenal world success of Munthe's book amazed even the author, and the need to account for it constantly obsessed him. Indeed he always maintained that he had dashed it off far too quickly. "I never for a moment thought it would be so popular, or I'd have written a better book." And he would often add: "I could have put in so many more chapters and improved the work! But I wrote it first and planned it afterwards."

He was perfectly sincere in all this, for fundamentally he was a stern self-critic. The only chapter in the book which he agreed was "not so bad" was the last, in which he describes himself facing his judges on Judgment Day.

He naturally had a colossal fan-mail, much of which he hardly had time to read. But complimentary letters from other authors obviously pleased him, although, or perhaps *because*, what is commonly known as literary ambition was foreign to him. For him, writing was not an end in itself, but a means of imparting himself to others, merely another outlet for his favourite occupation, giving. One of Munthe's greatest admirers was Rudyard Kipling, who wrote to congratulate him, adding that he, Kipling, envied him his literary talent. Both Kipling and Paul Bourget advised him seriously to give up medicine and take to writing.

When Munthe attended the same parties as that fiery wit Bernard Shaw, verbal duels were sure to follow. But at a breakfast given in London in Munthe's honour by the R.S.P.C.A., Shaw, replying to a speech by Munthe, declared that Munthe's insistence on the need for the protection of animals was good and to the point, and that he only hoped that this world-famed animal-lover would crown his life-work by founding a " Society for the Protection of Mankind ". " On all sides," he said, " I notice the most thorough, concientious and systematic schemes afoot to exterminate the human race." This was in 1934.

After every London season Munthe would return home with one or two new human ' discoveries '; it might be the cultured Chinese Ambassadress, a rediscovered friend of his youth, or even a woman who had started life as the wife of an English colonial officer, surrounded by head-hunters, and was now Her Highness, the Maharani of Sarawak, occupied in writing her memoirs. The pretty little Chinese Ambassadress charmed Munthe most, and her parting gift to him, a spectacle case inlaid with pink quartz, long held a place of honour on his writing-desk.

Another of his literary fans was the well-known English critic and *Times* contributor, E. J. Dillon. Munthe wrote to

him, asking him to explain the " puzzle " of *San Michele*'
success. Dillon replied: " Although by no means over
diffident, I know I am not clever enough to analyse and
pontificate on the almost magical power of your literary art
Your attitude to the world in general is ironical and tolerant—
and this is the basis of true humour, which is as rare today a
the miracles of old. The process of creative writing is itsel
something of a miracle, but a miracle which is manifest to
all. . . . And you seem to achieve your effects without
effort. Your capacity for harmonizing with and capturing the
spirit of all things, even where it appears to be least revealed
gives you a power which attracts all readers irresistibly. . .
This is my own feeling, and I know that others felt the same
You enliven almost everything you describe by pointing out
what is fresh, vital and strange in all the seemingly grey, lifeles
objects which surround us."

Munthe liked praise and appreciation as much as anyone
especially if he felt they were sincere. Spontaneous response
from grateful hearts meant more to him than expert criticism
favourable or the reverse, from literary critics or genera
readers, friends or even acquaintances. He was on a visit to
Sweden when he received a letter and a present from two
total strangers, which so moved him that he broke his usual
" grateful silence " habit and for once wrote an answer, which
not knowing the writers' identity, he was forced to publish
in a Swedish newspaper. His letter is worth quoting:

" During my three weeks' stay in Sweden I have received
an extraordinary number of letters from strangers in every
walk of life, literally hundreds of them, old and young
rich and poor alike. School children write to say that they
have opened their bird or squirrel cages and released their
former victims; hardened big game hunters have, it seems
discarded their rifles, and dog-owners resolved never again

o say a harsh word to their four-legged friends; young
women have written begging to be allowed to read aloud
o me; well-meaning, respectable parsons' wives have sent
ne old-fashioned cures for insomnia, and fortune-tellers
mysterious ointments for curing eye affections. I never
imagined that *The Story of San Michele* had so many admirers
in Sweden.

"A large percentage of these letters were anonymous.
Anonymous letters are the most interesting to a psycho-
ogist, and tempt me to break my principle of 'grateful
silence' far more than any signed ones. Indeed, the mere
thought of getting another letter like the one which Albert
Engstrom read aloud to me in Sven Hedin's library a few
hours before I left Sweden almost fires me to write another
book.

"The letter in question was signed 'An old maid'—just
that. If the 'old maid' had given her name and address
I would not have troubled to reply.

"Here is the gist of the 'old maid's' letter. When she
saw in the papers that I was in Solliden she and her lady
companion, Inga-Lisa, decided after much thought to send
the author of *San Michele* a present, 'in token of gratitude
for his kindness to birds'; this present was a pillow-case
which Inga-Lisa had embroidered for her mistress years
ago—it had never been used and lay stored away in a chest.
Now at last it was taken out, scented with lavender, carefully wrapped up in tissue paper and sent off with a letter
in a large envelope.

"Inga-Lisa had stitched a few birds on to the white linen,
which toned very nicely with the rest of the embroidery,
and had added underneath, as a finishing touch, the two most
beautiful words in our language: GUD'S FRED [God's Peace].

"Thank you, 'old maid', for your touching letter and
charming present, which has rejoiced my heart far more

than my book could possibly have rejoiced yours. And thank *you*, Inga-Lisa, for the birds on the pillow-case. May they chant to me in my dreams when I lay my restless head on your pillow. And tell your mistress from me that her anonymous old companion, whom I picture sitting beside her now in the lamplight embroidering another pillow for her 'old maid', is a far greater artist than I, for all the public adulation I receive. And tell her as well that there is more wisdom and true philosophy in the two words her old Inga-Lisa embroidered on the pillow-case than in all the empty verbiage of my *San Michele*.

"You might also add that you are a far better doctor than I, who have spent fifty years of my life in vain research work for drugs to relieve suffering and prolong life. Inga-Lisa, you are cleverer than I—you have a cure for everything. AXEL MUNTHE.

San Michele, September 1931."

Munthe went his own way, caring little for public opinion. This naturally made him a target for abuse and attack. In Germany, for instance, he would be criticized for his political views, elsewhere on the purely personal grounds of envy or spite. But he always seemed to take these attacks for granted. "Anyone who appears, ever so little, above the heads of the crowd must expect to be a target for blows," he would say. And then he would quote a verse which he vowed he had found somewhere in Goethe, and which seemed to clinch the matter:

> *Es bellt der Spitz aus unserm Stall*
> *Und will uns froh begleiten*
> *Doch seiner Stimme lauter Schall*
> *Beweist nur — dass wir reiten.*[1]

[1] "The little dog yaps from the stable yard
And wants to join in the hunt,
But his distant yappings merely prove
That we're riding away ahead of him."

THE ASCETIC

" A worn-out old camel can carry as much as half-a-dozen donkeys," was one of the Doctor's favourite retorts to people who tried to persuade him not to overstrain himself.

Though not over-robust, he started at an early age to discipline his body to his will. But only a man of good, tough material could have endured the succession of breaking-tests he imposed on himself. It was thanks to this native toughness that though he had several internal haemorrhages at various stages of his life his lung finally healed; none of the modern treatments was applied; merely the somewhat drastic one which he used on himself. Later in life he caught typhoid in Capri, where trained nurses were almost impossible to get. He remained unconscious for days. Then the fever left him, and all he could remember of his illness was a hazy notion of someone stealing into his room while he lay prostrate and snatching from his bed-table a beautiful gold coin engraved with the head of Tiberius.

By way of convalescing he prescribed for himself one of the Alpine mountain tours so fashionable at that time, from which he returned with frostbitten feet.

Munthe certainly had great reserves of physical strength, but his marvellous powers of endurance really derived from his strength of mind and iron will. Even in his later years, when a car ran into him and knocked him down in a London street, he got up and walked quietly home, afterwards fainting away from the pain of his injuries. Another such incident occurred when he was already almost blind; he fell down the whole flight of steps which led from the little verandah in Materita to the garden below. For weeks afterwards he could only walk with a stoop, and could hardly lie down, but it was months before he would allow himself to be X-rayed in London, when he was found to have broken several ribs.

The Man

He always preferred to walk whenever he could, and train or car journeys always made him restless. He would walk from the Stettin railway station in Berlin as far as the Swedish Embassy, which was then in the Tiergartenstrasse, on the plea that he needed exercise to refresh him after the train journey. The last part of the walk led through the Siegesallee, with its rows of Wilhelminian statues; these appealed to his sense of the ludicrous, and he would remove his hat and bow in mock solemnity to each of the figures in turn. This piece of foolery would remind him of the genuine sense of awe which he had felt on first seeing a camel, and which had impelled him to bow to it as he now did to the statues. "It looked so incredibly noble and distinguished."

When his sight began to fail and he had to give up his usual long, climbing expeditions on Capri island, he would stride every day for hours up and down the Materita terraces, with his loose weather-proof cape over his shoulders, and on his head one of his shabby old hats to shade his eyes. But even these perambulations did not satisfy his restless spirit. His mind must be occupied as well, and he would make his secretary Natasha or a friend follow him about reading aloud to him either *The Times*, some Swedish newspaper, or a book, usually Goethe, Heine, Dostoevsky, Carrel, Stefan Zweig, or some modern French author such as Pierre Benoit.

He could be seen in all weathers striding up and down under the oaks and olives of Materita, listening to the reading, asking questions or even alone with his dogs; if wet, clad in a hat and overcoat, if fine in one of his nondescript suits. Those old suits of his exactly fitted his simple mode of life at Materita. They may also have had happy associations for him; in any case he hated parting with them. In fact he never would part with them unless some " down and out " needed a rag or two to conceal his nakedness. Once, for instance, he entered a small Neapolitan inn, and began talking to the ' regulars '. They were chattering over their wine and delighted at the way the stranger kept joining in the conversation, and in out-and-out Neapolitanese, too. When he finally got up to go everyone called out " Addio, Signore."

" Why d'you call me Signore?" Munthe asked. " Surely we're all equals here!"

Everyone laughed.

" No, no," shouted someone, " only a Signore would dare to be seen in a shabby old suit like that!"

Tireless walker that he was, Munthe would venture out in all weathers. Once, after a walk in the London rain, he returned drenched to his flat and put his dripping hat and sodden boots to dry before the open coal fire. Soon a strong acrid smell began to spread through the whole flat, and Munthe's servant only just managed to save the hat and boots from being completely charred. The hat had a hole as large as a finger in it while one of the boots was singed and the other burnt almost to a cinder. But Munthe kept the hat and the singed boot all his life, and had the other boot entirely remade by a Capri cobbler.

Munthe did not actually demand of others an equally Spartan mode of dress, but if he noticed any friend or acquaintance wearing new clothes he would often remark slightly acidly: " How smart!", adding in the case of men: " *I* couldn't afford anything as grand as that!" This was not a pose on his part; the idea of indulging in any form of personal luxury was so alien to him that he could genuinely describe himself as " poor ". " The money we own is not ours to do as we like with." This was one of Munthe's favourite maxims, and it was no mere parrot-cry. It was true in more than the ordinary sense—in the sense which is rarely found either in life or literature, of practising what you preach.

Munthe only liked thick, practical, hard-wearing clothes. In his many walks in the old town of Stockholm he had discovered a shop where he would buy clothes whenever he urgently needed any—a shop which he was always recommending to his friends, diplomats and members of the Court not excluded. The shop was a seaman's outfitters. Munthe was Spartan not only in his clothes but in all his habits. He considered toothpaste an unnecessary luxury; ordinary chalk, he declared, was equally good and very much cheaper.

It was the same with his food. Munthe's meals were simple and frugal in the extreme, and the only luxury he allowed himself was an occasional bottle of wine. When he was staying with the King of Sweden he once asked a friend to go out and bring him back a cheap bottle of red wine. In Sweden you cannot get even tolerably good red wine cheap, and the Doctor, who was a connoisseur of wines, was disgusted with his friend's choice. The incident happened to reach the ears of the King's wine-butler who immediately fished out of the palace cellars a bottle of really first-class wine, and sent it up to Munthe's room. Munthe asked the price and at first insisted on paying for it. The King himself, in fact, could hardly persuade him to accept it as a gift.

Munthe's invitations to lunch or dinner were often followed by: " I must warn you there's only macaroni." Someone lunching with him in Anacapri once asked him why he always regaled his guests with the same dish, a kind of hash composed of eggs, potatoes and vegetables.

" I'll tell you," he replied. " Whenever I entertain here I order our set banquet."

Munthe was neither a vegetarian nor a fruitarian proper, but he loved fresh fruit and vegetables. His diet consisted entirely of yoghourt, cheese, eggs and macaroni, supplemented once a week with meat or fish, which he would wash down with either milk or cheap Italian *vin du pays*. When he was still a youth he had learned moderation in all things—food, drink and dress—and it soon became a habit with him.

His Spartan mode of life was not dictated by any outside authority, but by some inner need. So his attitude to material things was entirely consistent with his natural self or with the self he had trained himself to be.

The shady precincts of Materita, with grass and vegetation growing up between the flagstones, in which garden merged imperceptibly into wilderness, oak thickets into olive groves, was a fit setting for this strangely contradictory nature, humble yet proud, part genius, part simple human being. Here, eerie beauty and earthbound simplicity combined to frame the solitary figure as he strolled along his own paths, sunk in a world of his own.

Occasionally he would rouse himself from his thoughts and gaze down on the world of his fellow creatures. He understood, pitied and felt indulgent towards them, but they no longer stirred his curiosity. The hermit of Materita had no illusions about human beings, and as the years passed he needed their company less and less. Many of his contemporaries, whose friendship he had valued, had died long ago, and existed now only in his fantasies. Very occasionally he would welcome visitors from the outside world in the shade of the olives; among these were the wife and children of the bailiff who managed Materita's fields, vineyards and olive groves, and whom Munthe confessed to having engaged merely because he was small and jolly, and had ten children into the bargain. Every now and then one could see a couple of labourers pruning olives or felling trees in the park.

Once, when two workmen were felling an olive, a hard piece of root flew out and struck the Doctor on the temple, which immediately began to bleed profusely. Seeing this, the younger man fled without a word. The elder, however, Munthe's friend, the stonemason Pasquale, stared blankly at the Signore, his face chalky white, stammering invocations to the Madonna. He was about to collapse when the Doctor, holding his handkerchief over the wound, went up to him, put his arm round him and held him up. The two of them managed to stagger to the kitchen, where the Doctor handed over the still dazed Pasquale to the staff and went off to brew him a cup of strong coffee.

Munthe's complete self-control was perhaps one of the reasons why not only the simple fisher-folk of Anacapri, but others who had heard of him only by repute, credited him with supernatural powers.

One day the bell on the big entrance gate to Materita rang unexpectedly, and Munthe's usual peripatetic reading was interrupted by strange cries of distress. "Only five minutes, Doctor, only five minutes," the moaning voice continued, until at last the Doctor himself walked out to the gate to see what was happening. Facing him in the gateway stood a well-dressed man, a complete stranger, who immediately started to harangue him:

"My fate is in your hands," he cried. "I've come a long way to see you because I can no longer find any solution—any way out. I've gone completely off the rails, and you're the only person who I think might be able to help me. I had to see you, because I'd sworn that if even you couldn't give me the courage to face up to things and struggle on, I'd commit suicide today."

The Doctor spent about half an hour closeted alone with the stranger. Then he escorted him back to the gate, and his guest as he took leave of him seemed a man transformed. In an ecstasy of gratitude—of worship almost—he grasped Munthe's hand, bending over it as though about to cover it with kisses.

"I've found what I came all this way for," he said. "I knew you were my only hope. I'm going straight home now, and my nearest and dearest will never know that it's only thanks to you that I'm still alive."

This incident impressed Munthe and made him wonder what gave people such tremendous confidence in him. Often in the past he had tried to account for this mysterious power of his. Who or what had endowed him with it? Was its source in the unconscious mind, which flows along permanently under the tide of consciousness?

What did these people want of him? He was himself ill, nearly blind and merely sheltering from the world in his old tower, in order to devote his last days " to the things of the spirit ", as he himself expressed it. That young Anacapri girl, for instance, who had had a shock and for a time become mentally unbalanced—why had she insisted on being brought up to Materita, declaring that there the air had a special healing balm, which would revive her—what had she meant?

The daily routine at Materita was almost monastic in its uniformity and austerity. Only occasionally did the Doctor allow his guests to share their host's frugal midday meal. In the evenings he always insisted on being left alone, and saw no one but his lady secretary, who would read aloud to him for an hour after supper, before he went to bed. After that no one dared make a sound for fear of disturbing his sleep, sufferer from insomnia that he was.

Only Munthe's very closest friends can begin to realize the stoic simplicity of daily life at Materita, or can truly sense, through the baffling contradictions of his character, how little pose and how much genuine feeling there was in him.

Writer of Books

WHEN AXEL MUNTHE DIED, A PROMINENT SWEDISH critic, Sten Selander, wrote: " Axel Munthe and Selma Largerlof are the only authors of Swedish origin who have achieved world-wide renown. Munthe's career as an author must be unique. As far as I can remember no one else has ever become famous suddenly on the strength of one book written forty years after his earlier efforts had passed unnoticed into oblivion. Add to that the fact that his book was written in a foreign language and one may well seek far and wide without finding a parallel."

This statement is an exaggeration. Years before *The Story of San Michele* was published, Munthe had been known and appreciated as a writer. Warburg had already written in his *History of Swedish Literature* about two of Munthe's earlier books, *Letters from a Mourning City* [1] and *Memories and Vagaries*, [2] " . . . they disclose a humorous and sensitive observer who can play beautifully with words. . . ." In fact, it is true to say that his articles for the Swedish newspapers, from Paris and Italy, had made him one of the most popular writers in the Swedish press of that day.

In later years, Axel Munthe used to admit that in his youth he had forced himself to write, for one reason only—to earn money. His practice, largely philanthropic as it always was, brought him in very little, and for many years he struggled

---

[1] (John Murray, 1887.) Now out of print but largely incorporated in *The Story of San Michele*. This was the only book of his not written by him in the English language.

[2] (John Murray, 1898.) Originally published under the title *Vagaries*. The current 3rd edition, which is in its 11th impression, contains a new Preface.

with financial difficulties which handicapped his work. This was no doubt one of his reasons for feeling so pleased when his books found a market in England.

In 1887 when overwork and illness still further reduced his resources, he wrote to Hugo Birger's father: " . . . thank goodness, I have managed to get my stuff published in England and they have paid me so well that I really think I can manage now until I am well again."

He had been lucky from the beginning and found a publisher who believed in his work and who had taken trouble to introduce it to a wide public. John Murray, head of one of the oldest publishing houses in England, had become his trusted friend and, ever after, Axel Munthe was to speak of him with sincere affection. It amused Axel's sense of the historical to reflect that the beautiful old house in Albemarle Street had been the publisher's headquarters in Byron's time and that the great poet himself, with his manuscripts tucked under his arm, had made his painful way up those same stairs, to call on the Murray of his day, working under the same roof, in the very same rooms which his descendant now occupied.

The book he had published in Sweden about the cholera in Naples appeared in English in 1887 under the title *Letters from a Mourning City*. The small and select public who would read that kind of book took it instantly to heart. *Blackwood's Magazine* wrote: " Our friend, and all Axel Munthe's readers, we feel, would like to belong to his circle of friends; himself and his private thoughts are the stuff of which this book is made. The cholera plague in Naples is only the accident which happened to bring him into the limelight of publicity. We lay down his ' letters ' with a strong feeling that we know him, have come to know him well but would like to know him better still. . . . He is a Scandinavian Sterne."

From now on, Munthe was to be equally well-known as a writer and as a doctor. In 1898, another of his books was published in English, *Memories and Vagaries*. The literary critic of *The Times* wrote: " The author's English, always clear and concise, is full of life and would be excellent even for a born Englishman. His understanding of the way the poor live, especially the poor in Italy, their heroism, their aspirations, their weaknesses, and their sorrows, he knows them all as perhaps only a doctor can know them, and a doctor, too, who has courage, intelligence and sympathy. . . . Though devoted to animals, he never becomes a sentimentalist. He is merely drawn to all creatures who are ill, suffering, or unhappy, whether they be animals in a menagerie, Neapolitans dying of the plague or the unfortunate Madonna Del Duo Camino whose short triumph was doomed to such a disastrous finish . . . . combine with all this a love of the sun, the sea and the mountains, and a rich sense of humour, we find before us a character both strong and gentle, good to look upon honestly, unpretentiously portrayed in this book."

Another critic, referring to the passages about Capri, wrote: " . . . . the island has so long been connected with Dr. Munthe's name—and his name and house with its priceless collection is so well known to countless Englishmen and Americans, that they will easily recognize the following description, which appeared some years ago in a book which was read throughout the country . . . 'The most beautiful house I ever saw in my life is set in the brow of the precipice of Anacapri. It is a dream house or else its owner rubbed a lamp, and a genie gave it him. There is nothing else like it in the world in these days, and few men would be worthy to have it and to live there. But I think from what I hear that the man who does live there is worthy of it all.' "

These books appeared in several English editions and in 1911 were translated into Italian by the Governor of Naples with a flattering foreword by the historian Professor Villari who was then Italian Minister of Education.

At 50 Albemarle Street, about 1938

In London

Assistants.

From a drawing by Hugo Birger
Published in 'Letters from a Mourning City'

Success abroad in foreign tongues did not make him forget his native Swedish. At Christmas 1909, Norstedts of Stockholm published his latest book and already by the new year a second edition was in the press. Stockholm's *Dagblad* wrote: ". . . as a lover of Italy, with profound knowledge of the country, and as a sincere man of medicine, he sets out with the best of all qualifications for the task. What further equipment could be needed—and yet how infinitely more he has to offer! A brave heart richly endowed, a highly cultured spirit, broad and clear ideas, a poet's visions, on top of all this, an irresistible charm, full of vigour, sparkling with fun, and boyish pranks, which lightly cloak a never far distant sorrow. His writing is sufficiently refined to allow of utter simplicity. . . . It may well not be everybody's book, not everybody will notice, much less understand, the passionate rhythm and magic in his still melodies. Not only his story about Don Gaetano, the organ-grinder in Paris, but the whole book is written for those who understand music. . . . Few pages are more tender and lovely than those which describe his return to his beloved island. In one of the boats of a party of homeward-bound coral fishermen, as he tells of the eager hopes, expectations and fears of the simple mariners, we see he has, unbeknown to himself, become one of them. His heart beats with theirs."

Red Cross and Iron Cross came next in 1917, supposedly from the pen of a doctor in France. What the book lacks from a literary point of view it makes up for by a passionate pity which glows through every page. The characters seem incomplete and drawn to type, but they serve well enough as a mouthpiece for the author's beliefs.

It was now that his failing eyesight was to interfere more seriously with his manner of life. Despair began to take hold of him and his pen lay idle for years, while he gradually learned how to live like the blind. Not until 1927 did he write again, and again he wrote in English. Desultorily the book progressed to a finish—*The Story of San Michele*.

Sir John Murray used to say that it was due to Munthe's blindness, which caused him to buy an old typewriter, that the book was born at all. His blindness made him learn to type, but typewriting takes practice, so for practice he typed his thoughts and memories in the hope that this would teach him in time to write a reasonably legible letter.

The first edition appeared in April 1929. By July a second edition was already on the way. The third appeared in October and from then on the book pursued its triumphal way through the entire civilized world. Edition after edition, in one more outlandish language than the other, until Munthe told me, the year before his death, that he believed the Arab translation brought the book to thirty-seven different tongues.

In Sweden, though his old publisher had turned down the offer of a Swedish version of *San Michele*, literary circles quickly adopted this fashionable English book which naturally had a special appeal to Swedes. From the Queen's Villa in Rome, Munthe writes in November 1929: "I am pursued by six Swedish publishers, for the rights to a Swedish translation of a book I published in English this spring. Bonnier has despatched here two ladies to translate the book under my supervision, but I have sent them home again as I have no time to occupy myself with such work, and there are indeed, anyhow, more than enough books published in Sweden. Bonnier has offered me ten thousand crowns for a first edition and four thousand more if I will let him publish it first in the *Vecko Journalen*, a very high price for Sweden. But I have no literary ambition and I would in any case never consent to be Princess Marie's successor in this paper. The book is already in its fourth edition in England, and the American edition is doing better. A new edition of ten thousand copies is just coming out. So much the better for the animals who get the money."

As I have already pointed out, Axel Munthe was appreciated as an author at an early stage of his career, but there can be no doubt that it was *San Michele* which made him into a world figure. How and why the book achieved such fame is curiously difficult to answer, even if one assesses at its highest value the undoubted quality the work possesses. Probably the very form in which his story is told has something to do with it. His earlier books were written in the form of essays on travel, and as such always appealed to the fairly exclusive public who were able to travel in those days. The same can be said about most memoirs which on the whole have a fairly limited appeal. *San Michele* seems to occupy a category all its own somewhere halfway between travel and memoirs, a blending which the wider public liked.

The author is not one to revel in sensational disclosures about himself and his innermost soul. Nor is he the kind who seeks to wrap himself in an awe-inspiring veil of mystery. Most people who pick up the book feel in some sort of way that the book was written expressly for themselves. It is written by a very human person who has not made any effort to seem original or striking. The reactions he describes in the various episodes of his life are those of a straightforward, very understandable creature. He has been deeply moved by sights and impressions, and has found a remarkably efficient manner of letting others share in them. So his manner of writing necessarily becomes living and evocative. But even so, more than most writers, Axel Munthe managed to convey zest for life and warmth of feeling by the written word. His subject matter was no doubt as colourful and picturesque as any author could wish for, but that never prevented him, if he thought some scene still lacked life, from illuminating it with his own inexhaustible fancy. He never seems to have noticed when he crossed the border-line between the realms of fancy and reality. One of the greatest charms of *San Michele* surely lies in that continually recurring mixture of stark burlesque, reality and full-reined flights of imagination. In this way he created a world real enough for any reader to recognize his whereabouts while at the same time marvelling that the colour should seem brighter, the sun warmer, the pulse quicker, than in the humdrum life of everyday.

From the point of view of style, the original version in English is altogether more accomplished than the Swedish version written later. In his youth, his Swedish writing could at times be over-flowery. No hint of this appears in *San Michele*. Although his amazing sense of the finer shades and meanings of English words is proof enough of his complete mastery of the language, perhaps the fact that it was nevertheless a foreign language to him accounts for the remarkable and artistically valuable restraint which distinguishes his English writing. And yet this restraint never detracted from the poignancy of the scenes he described. What an arresting picture he produces with these few lines " . . . a couple of days later I was standing by his side in the coulisses of the Grand Opera watching Mademoiselle Yvonne dancing a pas de quatre, smiling on the sly at her lover whose flaming eyes never left her. We had late supper in the elegant little flat Maupassant had just taken for her. She had washed off the rouge from her face. I was shocked to see how pale and worn she looked compared with when I had first seen her in the yacht. She told me she always took ether when she was dancing; there was nothing like ether for a pick-me-up; all her comrades took ether, even Monsieur Le Directeur du Corps de Ballet himself—as a matter of fact I saw him die of it many years later in his villa in Capri."

Axel Munthe was a born narrator, a raconteur *par excellence*. He could devil out the essentials from any laboured and involved story, and with unerring precision sharpen them to a point that never missed the mark. He never let the details get the better of the contour. He thrived on story telling, and what he enjoyed doing, he did well.

He had the gift of giving atmosphere and temperature to his scenes, and full-blooded roundness to his characters. There is nothing vague or half-defined about his people or his animals; one can see them through their very skin or fur. How intensively the reader is made to sense the air in the still northern twilight when the sun sets in a golden red sky behind the ice-blue mountains of Vasso Jarvi: the Laps returning to their huts, the men with lassos swinging from their shoulders, their women-folk carrying fresh milk in the birch-bark baskets on their backs. Just as powerful is his pen when he tells of the sun-drenched islands in the Gulf of Naples and of the people who live there. He painted with a broad brush and a generous supply of colour, sharp contours and firm lines. Perhaps that is why his pictures are not easy to forget.

This power to make tangible, breathing creatures was to grow stronger as his power of sight grew weaker. When he was blind to the outer world, the inner one he conjured up for himself and his readers became more vivid and sensuous than ever before. To one who loved nature, mankind, animals and all life so keenly, blindness must have come as a crushing blow. For him who knew how to enjoy the lights and shades of this world, the subtly changing climate of all the things he loved best, the sudden loss of his eyesight must have been tantamount to death. And yet it was typical of this buoyant tough nature that he should manage to discover other values which made life still worth while. He even said he liked being blind. Though clearly this again was one of his exaggerations, it is probably true that his blindness did help him to write at his best. No longer could he be distracted and tempted by life around him, and undisturbed he was left to himself to gaze back on the only thing still left to him to gaze upon—memories. As he sat there with his typewriter alone in his tower, turning the eye that did not see to the blue water he knew so well, he could concentrate his full powers on the incidents in his long life as, one by one, they came back to visit him.

None of this, however, can quite explain the spell which *The Story of San Michele* seems to hold over the reading public. The astonishing influence which that book has had on all sorts of people in nearly every part of the globe, will probably remain a mystery and a subject for speculation for years to come. But astonishing though this may be, it certainly cannot be said to diminish the author's undoubted achievements.

Unlike other world-famous books, it has not yet, at the time of writing, shown any signs of losing its grip on the public imagination. Nor is its popularity declining. When Axel Munthe's death was announced over the wireless by the B.B.C. his English publisher was invited to speak a few words. Referring to the book of *San Michele* he mentioned that it was selling even better then than when it first appeared. In England alone, nearly a million copies had been sold. After twenty-three years, it is still regularly reprinted. It must have a curious and altogether unusual appeal.

Up to the day of Axel Munthe's death, and for many months after, unknown admirers in every corner of the world wrote him letters. Some begging for advice in sickness, some for money, some for the pleasure of telling him how much his book had affected their lives. On the whole this correspondence caused him more annoyance than satisfaction, for he had no means of dealing with this flood of letters, and most of them remained unanswered, many hundreds even unopened. " Glance through this heap," he would sometimes say to me, " in case there is anything special." By " special ", I soon discovered he meant a letter from some school-child writing in deadly earnest. To these, he nearly always replied.

It was amazing to see what some people would find to write about. One old woman in France wrote to send him a banknote, asking him to touch it, and send it back to her, for she had heard that all he touched would turn into gold.

In America his popularity was just as great though often combined with a very hazy notion of his true identity. Each time I visited America on my own business, I was to meet people whose extreme attention and deference towards myself at first surprised me, until I discovered that they mistook me for my distant cousin. On one occasion when I had gone over there to arrange for an exhibition of American art in Stockholm, I was much pleased and flattered to receive a request for an interview from a very prominent newspaper. The reporter arrived at my hotel and turned out to be a lady of uncertain age, who gazed into my face with wide open shiny eyes. She asked me every conceivable question about Italy, Sweden, the Royal Family, in fact everything except my exhibition. Finally her interest and admiration seemed to give place to grave doubt and even suspicion as she interrupted me—" Tell me, how is it possible that a man of your age can have experienced all the things you write about in your books. I believe it's all invented."

Many clever writers are incapable of conveying their art through the spoken word. Not so Munthe; his powerful charm worked just as successfully in conversation as in the pages of his books. I have never met a more fascinating talker. His phenomenal memory, aided occasionally by his imagination, was able to select at random from his experiences of close on ninety years, and produce no rambling reminiscences but stories relevant and sharply defined.

Perhaps more than most men, he could say with the ancients, " there is no human trait which remains unknown to me ".

This thorough knowledge of human nature enabled him to draw those penetrating likenesses; not always entirely flattering; often pricked out with very sharp highlights, sometimes downright ruthless. It amused him now and again to shoot an arrow dipped in a very potent, if not a deadly, bane. There were people he liked, others he could not stand, and often it was the latter who were most fun to talk about.

World Citizen and Man

FOR THOSE ADDICTED TO CLASSIFYING THE OBJECTS OF their studies, and neatly disposing of them in one or other category, Axel Munthe must present something of a problem.

He was born in Sweden and died in Sweden, and intermittently throughout his life he visited that country. To that extent he was a Swede. But it is well known that he sought British nationality. He established his house and planted his family in England. He wrote his best books in English and his most famous book was published first in London. He worked with the British Army on the Continent in the First World War, and his two sons fought as British officers in the Second World War. So as an author he came from England.

And yet the whole basic structure of his work as a doctor was laid in France. It was at the Sorbonne of Paris that he first qualified for practice, and at the Salpêtrière that he first discovered, under the guidance of the great Charcot, the latent powers that were to make him a world-famous healer. It was in France again that he formed his first circle of clients and built up his reputation. As " Doctor " Munthe he came from France.

But it was in Italy that he settled and worked to the fullness of his capacity. There it was he earned his lasting fame in the field of medicine. Naples claimed him as her son and bore him eternal gratitude. Rome provided him with a wealthy practice which enabled him to give his skill free to his poorer friends in the south. Capri gave him the materials with which to build what he felt to be his home. In Italy he lived the adventures that later became the stuff of which *The Story of San Michele* was made, the story that spread his name throughout the civilized world. By adoption then he was Mediterranean.

National frontiers were never to be very apparent to him and he felt equally at home when talking in any of five European languages. This immense facility was natural to him and in no way a pose, for it never deserted him even when sick and weary. Though he probably never thought about it, and certainly never spoke about it, he seems to have taken Europe for his parish and the world for his horizon.

To draw a quick likeness of a man whose nature takes on so many different aspects cannot be easy. Throughout his life he managed to maintain the impressionable nature of a child. His mind, always receptive, retained as the years went by the impression of each new experience as freshly as though he were still young.

Through his imagination he lived in two worlds, of which, certainly in later years, the largest and most enticing was the one within himself, and his blindness, which increased the weight of memory, strengthened the walls of his private world against encroachment.

Those who love music can best understand what rôle that can have played in his inner life. He was brought up as a child in a home where music was important. The violin-playing father, the wild, artist sister Anna with her beautiful singing voice, were themselves offsprings of the older home where Jenny Lind had found her first patron. The music he loved best was that of Schubert and Mozart, but another side of him was moved deeply by the dramatic music of Wagner. He never studied music as a performer, but he loved to sit at the piano and play by ear. His cousin Frederick wrote in 1896: " . . . at times his conversation and his whole intelligence seemed engulfed in a quagmire of the blackest hypochondriac despair for humanity. If at such moments one irritated him into a real rage he would do what no amount of persuasion could otherwise bring him to do—he would sit down at the piano and strum, violently, but with facility and an amazing memory for melody. As the music melted into harmony, so did his emotion. Schopenhauer would be allowed to rest at last."

Axel Munthe was undoubtedly an artist in the broad sense of the word. He knew how to appreciate art in most of its forms. In the end he came to find that the written word was the form in which he could best produce his own art. But it is easy to imagine him using some other medium of expression had his life taken a slightly different turn, for he had great aptitude in a number of spheres and was in no sense a " specialist ".

Like many of artistic temperament he had little real under-standing for the practical side of life. The world in general believed him to be very rich. Certainly a large amount of money passed through his hands, but the truth remains that throughout the greater part of his life he was short of money. His rich clientèle in Paris and Rome paid him lavishly and he spent all he got immediately on his infinitely larger practice in the slums of Europe. What was over was then spent on San Michele and Materita; and they were created with taste and knowledge but very little worldly wealth. Munthe never saved or put aside in safe investment. The extra-ordinary success of his book could, of course, have made him a rich man, for the book produced enormous royalties all over the world.

He used to maintain that he had not spent a farthing of the income from *The Story of San Michele* on himself. This may or may not be correct but, in addition to the birds who benefited from all the royalties on the early editions, there can be no doubt whatever about the army of needy persons in every walk of life in most countries of Europe who looked to him for assistance year after year, right up to the end of his life.

He followed no hard and fast rule as to how he should give his help. To some he gave it in kind, to others in money, to some he would hand over the future royalties of one of his books in one or more languages—a handsome gift as it turned out in the case of *San Michele*. To each he tried to give according to his or her needs—as he saw them. He studied their tastes and weaknesses with understanding and tolerance. He divided his resources fairly evenly between mankind and animals. If he was to derive any personal satisfaction from his donation he would usually require that two conditions should be fulfilled. The idea must originate with himself; and the gift must be anonymous. These two conditions were not always fulfilled, but it is true to say that most of his philanthropic work was done in anonymity.

How much money was spent in this way would have been very difficult to estimate were it not for the fact that when he died he left behind him little more than was needed to cover the many legacies he had willed to animals and friends.

Another characteristic of most artistic natures is their carelessness in matters of dress. Axel Munthe acquired, at any rate towards the end, a more than usual capacity for monumental disarray. He would wander about in the oddest collection of haphazard-looking old garments. His hats defied description, shabby, crushed, worn to holes. But, as he would say, holes let in air, which is good for the head. How much of this attitude was due to complete lack of personal vanity and how much was a kind of arrogance—take me as you find me or else for goodness' sake leave me alone—no one can say. Some people, who took perhaps a superficial view of this trait, assumed it to be the pose of a selfish old man who wanted at all costs to attract attention to himself. That he was an egocentric is certain, but he was not a selfish man. His worst enemy could never say that of him and it was, in fact, only other egocentrics who took that view. They hated his endless grumblings over his disabilities and they envied his sovereign disregard for convention and other people's convenience. But the disabilities from which his body came to suffer may well have seemed all-engrossing to him when they prevented his will from working its wonders any longer.

His mind longed in vain, after his eyes and hands refused, to set down at least two more books, the *Life of Victoria of Sweden*, and *Death and the Doctor*—both subjects on which he surely had much to say. Even his overbearing manner was not so unnatural in a man whose influence had made itself so strongly felt. What he wanted was for the good of others and no minor considerations must delay his purpose. He complained equally of delay caused by others or by himself, through his own shortcomings, his asthma, his blindness, his failing body, his ever-approaching appointment with Death. They grieved him sorely, all of them, and especially the last.

In the final analysis one comes upon the truth: Axel Munthe was always struggling to find a philosophy of life in which his whole being could trust. He made repeated attempts to adopt the Christian philosophy, but he could never do so wholeheartedly. Doubts assailed him every time. Perhaps he drew most inspiration from the philosophy of Schopenhauer. Even at the very end he returned to ponder over those works: but still he remained at heart what he always had been—an unhappy man who never completely succeeded in harnessing his conflicting powers and hitching his brilliant chariot to one great star.

It was this misfortune which showed itself in his failings,

his particular style of unconventionality, his sardonic humour and the ragged clothes, which were mistaken—often by people who themselves had much in common with him—for traits of egoism and posing which they secretly suspected in their own make-up. An example of this is the letter of the great Norwegian playwright Björnson to his daughter. From Rome in 1894 he writes of him: " . . . he dwells in the house, at the foot of the magnificent steps of the Piazza di Spagna, where once Keats the English poet lived, with Shelley in the rooms above. On entering Munthe's apartments, Keats' and Shelley's works lie around negligently as though by accident. The bindings are the most elegant imaginable. A prodigious dish stuffed with important-looking visiting cards meets one in the hall. Gladstone's card is on top. One assumes of course he called on Munthe yesterday. Dr. Munthe drives around either with a pair of thoroughbreds or with two Shetland ponies. Beside him in the carriage sits either the Crown Princess of X or his two dogs—one small, one enormous—both bred from the purest English pedigree kennels. The small one sits on the carriage seat: the big one sits on the bench with his back to the horses. On the box beside the coachman sits a footman, both in livery. Munthe himself, on the other hand, is dressed as plain as Napoleon. No one has ever seen him wear his decorations, not even gloves.

" By the merest chance, one might even say unwittingly, he drops a word here and there disclosing how invaluable he has been to the Queen, to the Crown Princess, Princess Ruspoli, the American millionaire's son, or touches, *en passant*, on the sad case of the British Ambassador (Lord Vivian) who died out here last year after many long consultations which proved Munthe alone right, and the other doctors all wrong. All this is said as spontaneously and with as little apparent premeditation as though we might say we have had lunch already, or we've taken coffee already. For one single visit he can earn as much as fifty or a hundred lire or even more. The money lies about all over his rooms, crumpled and forgotten in odd corners. Often of course he accepts no fee at all, which is no more than he should do . . ."

What a curious contrast between this picture of a worldly man in Keats' house with Gladstone's visiting-card on top in a dishful of grandees' names, driving down the Corso in a dashing turn-out, with spanking horses, liveried servants and all—and the slum doctor groping through the narrow dark alleyways, sitting through the last nights of the consumptive barrel-organ monkey's life, warming its milk. A curious case of split personality.

Munthe's first association with Björnson appears to have been one of literary collaboration in Paris; for in a letter recently discovered at Oslo University Björnson writes to F. W. Hegel on February 25, 1887: " . . . When I started this story I was already heavily involved in another which I have been working upon for some time. It is called ' On God's High Road ' and is in the main a doctor's yarn; a priest and a doctor who meet over the beds of the sick and dying in a hospital. They are friends, they were school fellows. I am working on the material with Dr. Munthe, a young but very learned and experienced Swedish doctor; he became enthusiastic when he heard the outline of the story and could not understand why I had not already made use of it long ago. As I said, I laid it aside so as to write a *short* story for *Nyt Tidsskrift* (the new periodical). And then it all got completely out of hand: I had not realized what I was letting myself in for. . . ."

That two such egocentrics as both these men were to become should have been able to work in double harness is astonishing indeed. I have never heard Axel Munthe's views on Björnson, but to judge by the latter's letter to his daughter some years later, they seem to have parted with some ill-feeling on both sides.

As a sort of free-lance doctor, he was at times violently criticized by his colleagues who remained strictly within the sheltered confines of the medical profession. Swedish doctors hated this man who had deserted them in his very boyhood with only the sketchiest medical learning and then become famous after studying in France. His qualifications seemed to fit into no category. He seemed to have no recognizable label. They finally called him a " nerve doctor ". What he lacked in theoretical training he made up for in practical experience and it had to be admitted that he made many very remarkable cures. He invariably tried to belittle his own work, but the truth remains that in time it won him a reputation which far exceeded his fame as a fashionable doctor in Paris and Rome.

He used to maintain that he was no doctor just as he insisted he was no writer. This of course was a pose. His training as a doctor had been both intensive and varied: but more important still were his natural qualifications. The vital interest he took in his patients, his uncanny understanding of human nature, and above all his flair for diagnosis, were the fundamental reasons why he became a great doctor. He was able to penetrate to the very depths of his patients, and he seemed to have the power of imparting to his patients some of his own strength of will, so that they themselves joined him in an active effort to bring about the cure. This power was at times so strong that it amounted almost to hypnotism. Though there is no evidence that, as has sometimes been said, it was his practice to hypnotize.

In his private life, Munthe was the most unpretentious of men. He placed outward appearance at its lowest possible value. His personal requirements were simple in the extreme. Only when he drove this natural unpretentiousness to excess,

Axel Munthe with his son Malcolm and his grandson   Hilda Munthe

Axel Munthe. A drawing by William Rothenstein

often in self-defence against the pomp and trappings of the great with whom his life was largely surrounded, did he lay himself open to the very accusation that was often on his lips. His simplicity might then be mistaken for a pose, an outward trapping itself. But his contention was nevertheless sincere throughout: the great must be above self-indulgence, above all dependence on luxury. At heart he remained what he always had been, an unregenerate aristocrat.

He had physical courage. His life amongst the plague-stricken people bears irrefutable witness to this, so does his seeking for adventure on the dangerous mountains of Switzerland. He had moral courage too. He was always the first to admit his failures. He never wavered in the face of sometimes very adverse public opinion. He doggedly pursued his unconventional course.

He had above all a great heart, though he did his best to hide it under the heavy cloak of a cynical poseur.

His pity was almost inexhaustible and he extended it in the most unexpected quarters. He was not easily taken in. He knew people's weaknesses but nevertheless agreed to help, provided he saw something about them which appealed to his sympathy. Some of their weaknesses would amuse him secretly. I remember in recent times when a certain gentleman sought Munthe's help in the matter of obtaining for himself a position at Court. Munthe listened for hours, without a flicker of understanding on his immobile face, as the unhappy applicant tried to make the reason for his visit sufficiently apparent. He let his visitor flounder on, amused and anxious to see to what lengths he could go before finally coming to the object of the visit. In the end, and in quiet humour, he did help: but how different from the cases of real need where his help came swiftly and in the dark.

One day I asked him which of the many tributes he had received in the whole course of his career he valued most.

He pondered for some time and then told the story which some of his readers may already know. When he was a young man in Capri, Pacciale, a fisherman friend of his, lay dying. He was one of the truest and most pure-hearted of men. His wife and children had never known him to say an unfair word. The old priest had administered the Last Sacrament and now stood by the far side of the bed. Members of his family huddled silently in the shadows of the little room. Pacciale had fallen into a deep slumber and seemed to have left this world, when, slowly and for the last time, he opened his eyes. He gently stroked the hand of his doctor friend and whispered " Siete buono come il mare "—" You are good like the sea."

To many people the sea is hardly the personification of goodness. The sea is ungovernable, rough, and often cruel. But to the old fisherman who had lived all his time by the sea and on the rocks which came out of the sea, the great element had become all that the waving cornfield is to the country-man. It was his horizon, it had afforded him his living, it had given him his meed of adventure, hopes, fears, dreams.

Possibly he was right and no better epitaph could be found for Axel Munthe: he was good like the sea.

*   *   *

Towards the end, his thoughts turned to the future of San Michele.

In his talks with the Crown Prince of Sweden,[1] that keen archaeologist and amateur of all classic art, he learned about the activities of the Swedish Institute of Art in Rome. The Prince was its President, and its Principal was Professor Axel Boethius. Munthe then discovered that the scope of the Institute could be enlarged if it were possible to find a residence where Swedish scholarship students could live and work in the country of their studies.

[1] Now King Gustav VI.

A last donation

The idea of handing over San Michele to this worthy cause appealed to him. His mind worked on it day and night. Should he give it before or after his death? In the end he decided to leave it to the Swedish State in his will. By so doing he sought to preserve for posterity his home, with all its dreams for reviving the classic tradition of a simple and beautiful way of life.

His will is dated 16th November, 1948:

" I hereby declare in this my last will and testament, that I, Axel Martin Fredrick Munthe, bequeath my property called San Michele at Anacapri with all appertaining land and buildings, and with all the works of art, books and goods and chattels that may be found there at the time of my death, to the State of Sweden, for the purpose of encouraging the further growth of cultural relations between Sweden and Italy.

" It is my desire and hope that the State will entrust the Swedish Institute in Rome with this donation so that they use it for the furtherance of their aims. I am confident that the Institute will find the means and ability needed to ensure that, while retaining the present character of San Michele, the purposes I have indicated above may be put into effect, for instance by affording living accommodation for Swedish students, artists, archaeologists, journalists or other guests who may be considered to share my feelings for Italy and the classic civilization, as well as for classical research in general.

" I trust that, in carrying out the necessary alterations in San Michele the well-being of the persons at present looking after the property will be given due consideration.

" Signed,
" AXEL MUNTHE."

By this last donation he intended to give to coming generations in two countries the best he had left to offer. For the youth of Sweden, where he had been born and where he died, he hoped to introduce into their ultra-modern education the breath of ancient wisdom and culture which would teach them to reflect while they were still young that the eternal values were brought to perfection by the ancients in a world where labour-saving devices and luxuries had no place. To the Italians he hoped to introduce new friends from abroad who would respect and emulate the teachings of their classic ancestors, and who would learn to love the soil and the people of modern Italy.

Thus, at the last, he relinquished his San Michele.

The Last Years

THE GOLDEN CAGE

TRACING THE CROWDED WAYS OF HIS RESTLESS LIFE, IT IS not always easy to decide where to mark the stages of his long journey. But two milestones stand out clearly in the winding way. San Michele, romantically perched in brilliant evidence on the top of an arrogant cliff, surveying the view that an emperor scanned a thousand years before—to this place Munthe had come from the wearing toils of daily life and from the griefs and illnesses of the great cities where he worked. Here he came to recreate his burning spirit, plunging his thoughts into the glories of the past, preparing for some new assault into life. Here he constructed with his own strong young hands his dream of earthly paradise, here he lived the morning of his day.

And Materita, built to defend royal Naples of the Renaissance, crouching on the western slope down to the sea, there, behind its crumbling ramparts, he found refuge from his patients, from his friends, from his work, from his life, from the sun—a blind old man. There he lived the evening of his day—an evening luminous and lasting long into the night. There he wrote the story that was to outshine his earlier renown. Twenty years of life were still before him when he finished his greatest book.

It was the Second World War that finally obliged him to forsake even Materita. In restless haste, reminiscent of his old temper, he prepared to leave. Where to go? To England. First, to Stockholm to arrange some matters, then on. The first stage was completed. The King of Sweden

[195]

graciously invited him to the Palace, from where he was well placed to plan his further journey. But those plans, continuing and changing from week to week, from year to year, were never realized.

At first the war provided an excuse which covered up his faltering powers of decision. But the war ended and still Munthe remained with his kind host. He complained bitterly of having been so long cooped up in those old apartments of the Palace. But he could never decide to move. I do not know if perhaps he always suffered to a certain extent from indecision, but certainly it was so by the time I knew him. When summer came round he moved at first with the Court to the little summer palace at Solliden on the island of Oland: but the obvious need to be sociable at all times, and on parade most of the day, required too much exertion for one of his temperament, so he preferred to remain in the Palace at Stockholm, moving to rooms on the north side overlooking a cool garden with its fountains.

One summer he havered in miserable suspense, with the idea of moving to the old home at Leksand which had been his wedding present to his wife. Before the war he had made a brief stay there every year, as a pilgrimage, " to see it once again ". In the end, even that journey seemed too long and he consented, with much grumbling and testily reserving the right to change his mind up to the very last minute, to go to an hotel at the seaside resort of Saltsjobaden outside Stockholm for the hottest weeks of the summer. No sooner was the day of departure appointed than doubts as to its suitability would beset him, and once again the whole plan would be in the melting pot. All the patience of Job was needed by the kindly palace staff in supervising and finally completing the journey of the aged Doctor. At Saltsjobaden, he had a beautiful lofty room with its own private balcony, overlooking a wooded park with the sound of birds in the pine trees and the lapping of waves on the rocks beyond. He loathed every instant of his visit, having decided to loathe it from the moment he set out. In fact the only day his deep depression relented was on the eve of his return to the palace. There, the summer over, he could once again indulge his fancy for journeying to Capri, away from the fast-approaching northern darkness of autumn and winter. The bitter cold froze his lifeblood. He hated being deprived of his old haunts, his walks in the cypress garden amongst the acanthus leaves, the touch of the dogs, and the voices of his people at Materita. Autumn and winter were hard to bear. Perhaps the spring was the season that chafed him least. Spring seems mild in Sweden, after the snows have melted, but to Munthe it brought a warning of summer, and, for him, unbearable heat in Capri. So in early spring, for a moment, he was unable to wish himself elsewhere than in Sweden. But scarcely had the gentle air penetrated into his dark quarters in the palace when restlessness returned, and with it his feverish seething preparations and plans for the great journey to be undertaken at last, before a new winter should catch him.

He seemed to think that the nature of my work at the Swedish Travel Association qualified me, in some special way, to help him. He would telephone to me at every conceivable moment, asking me to come round to the palace to discuss his latest idea about travelling to Capri. He consulted any number of friends in Sweden and John Murray in London. He liked to compare their opinions. Tickets would be ordered for the same journey by different people on his behalf. And then they would be cancelled at the last minute. Munthe's journey became a sort of recurring nightmare for every travel bureau in the kingdom. Accustomed as he was to beginning at the top, he refused to trust the clerks or local branch managers of railway booking offices, but called for the Director of the entire railway organization. He wanted to make quite sure that there was not some train which could be persuaded to do the trip, Stockholm–Rome, without necessitating any change. He refused to accept, as sufficient excuse, the barriers which a raging war had built up around the Continent. When hostilities had ceased, the direct carriages from Sweden through to Italy were re-established. But by then it was too late.

There were two alternative railway journeys which he could have attempted. One, through Paris, breaking his journey there for an afternoon; the other through Switzerland, with a few changes in comparatively easy stages. Along either route, he had innumerable friends at different Embassies to whom he appealed for help and hospitality during the necessary breaks in his journey. In due course they one and all understood that he would never arrive, so they went on promising gaily to place themselves at his entire disposal whenever he wanted.

One of his staunchest friends and advisers through all these endless changes was the British Military Attaché in Stockholm, General Sutton-Pratt. With unfailing patience and good humour, as well as an unfeigned sympathy, the busy General would visit him in his spare moments.

When, periodically, Munthe reached the conclusion that sitting for long hours in a shaking train would be too much for him, he flung his whole enthusiasm into plans for air travel. The head of the airport was duly summoned and carefully sounded. The trouble seemed to be, would his old heart stand the altitude? Could a guarantee be given that the aircraft would not fly higher than a certain level approved by his heart specialist? He did not mind dying quickly anywhere, but slow suffocation in a heart attack on board an aircraft would be a miserable end, he thought. Everyone agreed. Oxygen masks were sent up to the palace for his inspection. He examined them gingerly with a faint grin on his face, which made manifest to the unhappy airman that he disbelieved in these boyish, half-baked inventions for providing a man of ninety with artificial atmosphere! Later, relenting, he said he would go with their new-fangled machine if only it did not start so infernally early in the morning. Why not sleep at Broma, the Stockholm airfield the night before? That idea appealed to him enormously; for days he toyed with it, allowing it to fire his imagination. In the end, he feared he would be unable to sleep through the noise of roaring engines in the night. No one could find an adequate answer to that. He would charter a plane which could come down at any point when he felt inclined to rest! But how? Supposing he wanted to come down when the plane was over Germany?

His Excellency Monsieur Guenther, the Swedish Minister Plenipotentiary in Italy, called on him one day and described a motor trip he had made to Rome. A brilliant idea! And one opening up to Axel Munthe's darkened perspective fresh fields flowering with possibilities for a totally new plan involving a totally new set of people! The directors and presidents of the Motor Association of Sweden were soon to wend their eager way to the Palace. Dispirited, the old man let them go quicker, even, than their predecessors. My own relief was considerable, for I had promised to drive him myself, and the thought of the long trip over the Alps, the succession of halts for rests, the wartime formalities at every frontier, the international petrol permits, the inevitable punctures, all filled me with foreboding and fear.

Wearily he rose again and turned to his first and last love, the sea. There were nice tarry-smelling cargo boats that plied between Stockholm and Naples, his very doorsteps. The directors of shipping lines arrived and sat in the same chairs the other gentlemen had occupied. There were indeed such cargo boats. Some of them were riding at anchor or tied to the busy quayside, at Skepsbron, below the royal palace walls. He could see them from his windows. But no, he could not. He called for cloak and both sticks, and, ably supported, he made his solemn way down to the sea to look at ships.

The commotion is now at an end, and one cannot help wondering why so much effort from so many people should never have resulted in getting him away to the island of his desire. I believe that one reason counted with him far more than the difficulties of travel, or the complication and discomfort of living in the old fortress of Materita with its primitive arrangements and its inaccessibility. Never far from his mind, I believe, was a great fear; the fear of having to cope with the accumulated problems of his many dependents and protégés, who so eagerly awaited the return of their immortal benefactor to Capri. The vision of a torrent of callers blackening the path to Materita; people who were unhappy or sick or mad or poor—they would all come as before, and they would discover that he could help them no more. And perhaps also, struggling against the desires of his conscious mind, there was a hankering to die where he had been born, in the boisterous northern clime rather than in the dreamy land of the sun.

*   *   *

In his last years he came to hate sincerely all the publicity that still dogged his footsteps. He longed for peace, but not always was he successful in securing it. In his writing-room, by his desk, a rug over his knees, he liked to be alone and unattended. The door into the corridor would be left unlatched so that those whom he called for could come in without causing him to rise to open the door. This arrangement at times, left him open to unexpected intrusion. A persistent and well-placed intruder could bluff his way past the sentries and palace porters right up to his rooms. It was not easy, then, to pretend to be " out ". A photographer from an American magazine caught him in his doorway in this way, and mercilessly took shot after shot, with his blinding flashlight camera, as his aged and defenceless prey sought in vain to beat a blind retreat. The result was two pages of sorry photographs which can have given pleasure to no one. This kind of publicity, which pretended to do public service by shedding light upon a world figure, in reality only sought greedily to earn an unworthy living for its perpetrators, at the expense of an old, tired, and disabled man.

In defence of Axel Munthe's memory, I have decided after some doubts to mention two instances which particularly distressed him in his old age.

A person whom he had considered as a friend took the opportunity, while escorting him during his lonely hours, of getting Munthe to talk intimately of the past, and then, without warning, or asking leave, published these unguarded utterances. It was no great feat to coax Munthe into an acid humour from which he would spit out at the world, friends and foes alike, all his pent-up anger at his golden cage. He tried to have the record suppressed, but failed and then asked my advice as to what to do. Finally I persuaded him that this kind of publication would only gain from any action on his part. So he bore it in silence.

Still more distressing to him were some articles, written in the more sensational sections of the press, claiming to have discovered in the archives of Nazi Germany correspondence between himself and Goering, shortly before the Second World War. The carefully selected passages from this correspondence were made to imply that Munthe was an admirer of the German Field-Marshal and interested in selling to him his property of San Michele. Well-meaning efforts to explain away these amazing disclosures pointed out that a man well over eighty years old might easily be forgiven for getting his political affiliations slightly mixed. Nothing, however, could be further from the truth. In spite of all his disabilities, Axel Munthe was entirely clear-headed and uncompromising in his political beliefs up to the last. His whole life had been devoted to the sick, the weak, the underdog. He had no love to spare for those who were satisfied with their racial superiority, worldly riches, or greatness, and in the Nazi grandees he saw no exception to his rule. He had firmly espoused the British cause against the German and never, on any occasion, made a secret of his ideas.

His sense of fairness and humanity made him regret in later years the lengths to which his passionate hate of the German ideals had driven him, in the period of the 1914–18 war, when he condemned the race wholesale in his writings. He attempted even to right the balance in a humane fashion by giving money for German soldiers blinded in the war. He was, also, frankly grateful to the Italian dictator Mussolini for agreeing to grant legal protection to the migratory birds who came to rest on his mountain at Capri, but he was never a supporter of the Fascist or the Nazi régime.

That the theatrical and, to Munthe's mind largely comic, Field-Marshal Goering should cast a longing glance at San Michele, erected on the foundations of a Roman Imperial home, is hardly to be wondered at. How fitting it must have seemed to this florid German to strut along the pavements that had borne the footprints of Tiberius! How typical of Munthe's sense of humour, to lead on this " great " man in his harmless if ridiculous ambition! Goering, the lover of pomp and luxury, in San Michele—the spartan little rock home, without water, sanitary or heating arrangements. The temptation for fun was irresistible, and, to give it all added spice, Axel Munthe, who spoke excellent German, conducted this correspondence with the tyrant of Europe throughout in English.

Ferreting for sensation with which to make a good headline, these newspapers sought to reveal to the world the hero of humanitarians flirting with the insane god of tyranny and they quickly learned the art of picking from their context words, phrases and passages which could be re-arranged to prove that Munthe had written what he never even thought. They achieved little enough, apart from hurting the feelings of a very old man.

EUTHANASIA

The old Greek word, euthanasia, was often on Axel Munthe's lips. It seemed to haunt him in later years as an old man, just as it had haunted him throughout his active career as a doctor.

The word has three meanings. The first and original one being, simply, the art of dying naturally. This meaning of the word has no special connection with medicine or the doctor's art; it is the concern of every human, in every walk of life; to be studied in good time before it is too late. Munthe, of all people, might have been thought to have learned this art from the sick and dying he had tended during nearly seventy years—the classic art of meeting death without fear, with dignity. But he admitted, honestly, that he himself feared death. In his early books, with all the recklessness of youth, he wrote that the pestilence and tortured deaths in Naples held no terror for him. But later, in *The Story of San Michele*, he told the whole truth. From the beginning to the end, he had been terrified by the thought of both. When I first met him, a few years before his end, he would often say, "I am afraid of dying. The thought of death haunts me in my sleepless hours. I have not finished with life; there is so much more to be done."

He used at times to persuade himself that it was not death he feared so much, but the process of dying. The slow, fore-doomed fighting of a battle that must be lost. The agony of a finished heart petering out in suffocation. Perhaps the real explanation lay in his failure to arrive at any conclusion that could satisfy him as to what follows death. At times he would ask, like some pathetic child, is there a life afterwards? To him, with his strongly individualistic and egocentric per-sonality, another life must mean a life in which his own personality could carry on as a recognizable, separate entity.

The resignation of the pantheists, the gradual elimination of self, melting into a sublime and undivided whole, could be only of little comfort to him. He was not a convinced Christian, but he used to try to find some good reason for believing in the Christian tenets. He would ask people his eternal question and, before they could reply, he would add with a sorrowful sniff, " —but never mind, you can't answer that ". If his visitor were hardy enough to say firmly, " Yes, I can ", he would listen and then with a shrug of an uncon-vinced shoulder he would mumble " —what can he know about it after all?"

Euthanasia can also mean the doctor's part in bringing to a more bearable and painless end the sufferings of the dying. It has been said that this was perhaps one of the secrets of Munthe's fame as a doctor. The art of curing real or imagin-ary petty ills was well known to him, and he practised it to earn money. But it is doubtful if he ever looked upon it as his vocation. The best in him was only called forth when he lived amongst the most unhappy creatures in the depths of their misery, men and women in southern Italy, the wounded in France, or the barrel-organ monkey dying of consumption. These he could always help. For these only he saved the absolute refinement of his art: and on these only he lavished it with both hand and heart.

On suicide

There is a third meaning to the word euthanasia, probably the most generally used today—the doctor's action in bringing a swift end to an illness which is protracted and hopeless. Munthe never doubted this to be part of the doctor's rights—he considered it his duty, without the quibbling formality of the dying patient's acquiescence. He freely admitted to making use of this right on many occasions. The question of a human being's right to end life in such cases interested him not only from the point of view of a doctor but in relation to suicide. Without putting his own conclusions into words, he would often consider with himself and with others the question of a man's right to end his own life. There can be little doubt that Axel Munthe believed in that right.

He sometimes told me of his talks with other people on this subject. Sailing with Maupassant and his friend Yvonne on their yacht *Bel-ami*—the tale is one of the most fascinating in *The Story of San Michele*—Maupassant asks him about death by drowning and Munthe explains that a man can meet death fairly easily that way. Years later he was to meet Stefan Zweig, the writer. In London shortly before they left Europe for Brazil, Zweig and his wife called on Munthe and discussed at length their plan of suicide, the morality of it, and the best means to carry it out. Zweig knew that Munthe had studied deeply the workings of poison, and could be looked upon as an expert in the matter. He and his devoted wife had long suffered the tortures of Nazi Germany and, after they escaped, found themselves unable to bear the remainder of their lives. Soon they were to end it.

Undoubtedly the same thought came to Axel Munthe. His delicate health from childhood onwards, his long period of blindness, his black despair, all go to explain how his mind came to think that way. Though in his own case his innate sanity eventually triumphed, he nevertheless wrestled with the thought, and with the instruments, too, of self-destruction.

I believe he wanted to hoodwink himself into the feeling that he was master of his own life, just to learn what it felt like, and if indeed it was possible.

His struggle with death was pathetic. He suffered acutely every time some new step in his decline became too obvious for him to conceal it from himself or his friends. When I came into the room, as he sat there, the old rug over his knees, he invariably said the same words, in that inimitable tone of voice—" Forgive me if I don't get up "—half irony, half earnest. He intended it, no doubt, as the usual form of courtesy, but equally he wanted to show that he could get up if he cared to try. The day I came and noticed that he no longer made his opening remark, I understood he had learned, and taken to heart, the tidings of one more defeat in the long succession of battles with the inexorable victor.

He remained himself right up to the end. Not until the beginning of the new year 1949, when his asthma suddenly turned to inflammation of the lungs, and finally took his remaining strength, did he abandon his will to live. The illness passed, and his old humour flickered once more, but it was the last effort. He was exhausted and could only throw off his slumbers for short minutes at a time. On the 11th of February, at three in the afternoon, he died, in his ninety-second year. Death had, after all, come as a friend. The long agony he had feared so greatly was not for him. At the end, though sickness and fatigue had left their mark, a look of peaceful and confident understanding seemed to rest on his curiously youthful features.

The End

"ONLY WHEN I'M DEAD WILL I STOP DYING, FOR LIFE for me now is merely a slow process of dying. I die during my sleepless nights, gasping for breath; beset by morbid imaginings, I die as day succeeds melancholy day. Friends pay me short visits, which cheer me for a while, but when they leave me it is as though Death, who has been a silent witness all the time, comes and sits opposite me again without a word. Death has entered my room through the window, and remained there, an invisible occupant.

"Death has followed me all my life and influenced all my actions—gently exhorting me to take time by the forelock and exploit the days while they were still mine.

"So for many years Death has walked with me and been my constant companion. Now I confess it frightens me less than when I was young. All I dread now is the actual process of dying and the prospect of a succession of days and nights of ever-increasing suffering."

Axel Munthe would often sit for hours at a time in his big armchair drawn up close to the window of his room in Stockholm palace, a prey to these morbid fantasies.

Seeing him sitting there one might have supposed him moribund, but his thoughts were ranging far and wide. In days gone by he had often quoted Montaigne: "When I rest my feet my mind also ceases to function", but during this period of apparent inactivity and lassitude he would be invaded by his thoughts, subject to the extremes of emotion; melancholy at times, at times indifferent, at times showing a friendly interest in the lives and occupations of the

[207]

various people who up to the end continued to visit him and to contribute to the picturesque pageant of his life.

On October 30, 1948, Munthe's ninety-first birthday, his room was transformed into a flower garden. The palace staff, the inhabitants of Stockholm, indeed the whole country had addressed congratulations and birthday presents to the small suite of rooms which had now become Munthe's world. He could get about very little now, and had to be supported by his guardian angel, Sister Brita, whom a kindly Fate had sent his way.

Sister Brita had come to look after him. Not because he was famous and a personal friend of the King. To her he was merely Axel Munthe, a man to whom she had taken a liking from the start. At first he found it hard to believe that an experience of his youth was to be repeated in his old age; that he was to meet another ' Sœur Philomène ', to care for and devote herself to him as only a woman can.

During the last months of Munthe's life Brita nursed him day and night. He invited her mother to stay in the palace with her, to allow her a few hours' rest from time to time.

Gradually Christmas Eve approached. A small Christmas-tree had been brought in to brighten the sad winter twilight which filled the old palace. With the approach of darkness the scent of the lighted candles was wafted through the rooms, and the Doctor asked his two guardian angels to lead him to the tree. Standing motionless in the open doorway, he solemnly took off his hat, which he always wore to protect his eyes from any form of glare, and gazed for some time at the blaze of light, lost in thought.

That was his last Christmas on earth. Early in the New Year he fell ill. He made one miraculous recovery with the help of penicillin, the new drug, and his sons, who had hurried from England to his bedside, were allowed to carry him from his bed to his sofa and to spend a few hours with him. At moments, in fact, he became quite lucid and joked with them, and this reassured them so much that they felt no qualms about returning to England.

But his strength was exhausted. His doctor soon began to diagnose cerebral haemorrhages, for his mind seemed to be constantly wandering and losing all sense of reality. But the nightmarish, feverish dreams which had disturbed his short moments of sleep during his first illness luckily did not recur. Once again in those first nights of his illness he had had visions of war, suffering and bloodshed, but also peaceful dreams of returning to his Ithaca after a long Odyssey, and his lips had formed broken sentences, uttered as in a dream.

But now his mind had become calm again. Death was approaching quietly. What Munthe had so long awaited came gently, and removed all that had so long tormented him. He had ceased to struggle for life, and lost all fear of death. Lassitude and a deep peace alone filled his heart before it finally ceased to beat. About three o'clock on Friday, February 11, 1949, Axel Munthe stopped dying.

His sons, who had returned from England, and the friends who first saw him dead found him lying serene and peaceful, the expression on his face younger by years.

Time and again he had insisted that his death should cause as little fuss as possible. He wanted neither cross nor tombstone on his grave. Indeed, he had hankered after a seaman's grave; the sea and its secrets had meant so much to him. In the words of a German poet he had named it " a grave fit for a King ". At any rate, he had insisted on there being no ceremonial or display of mourning when he finally departed.

The funeral was held on February the 17th in the Chapel of the Holy Cross in Stockholm. Munthe's coffin was lowered into the grave adorned with white Christmas roses, and the patch of cemetery ground which covered it was bestrewn with countless wreaths sent by friends from all over the world.

The End

At the foot of the coffin was a special wreath of dark bay leaves and white blossoms, with a blue and yellow ribbon imprinted with the Royal coat of arms and inscribed:

To my friend Axel Munthe in gratitude. Gustaf.

After Handel's Largo and the Litany the congregation sang an old hymn, which Munthe would often recite to himself, especially in his later years:

> As forest trees do wither
> When golden autumn's here,
> So may I likewise perish
>   Without fear.
> A better season cometh
> When forest trees are green,
> And may I likewise flourish
> In God's eternal spring.
>
> As birds migrate in winter
> To some far-distant clime,
> So may I take wing and fly
> From this world's snow and rime.
> Bird of passage lend me wing
> To fly to where the angels sing.
>
> As gay and light-winged butterflies
> Burst from their dark confine,
> So may the Lord lend wings to me
> To pierce through mine,
> That I who long in bondage lay
> May freedom find on Judgment Day.[1]

[1] A free translation of a Danish Song (by Ohlenschläger, 1813); now included in the Swedish Hymn-book, No. 572.

Index

Index

Index

Index

Index

Index

99